T0356204

What a blessing this book has been to me. Full of the truths of scripture, laid out in short devotional chapters that the whole family can use. Cathcart explains the Shorter Catechism in a way the young people can understand, and gives real life examples on applying the principles in daily life. He has also included challenging questions at the end that will promote profitable discussion. An excellent family devotional guide.

LINDA FINLAYSON
Author of *God's Timeline* and *God's Bible Timeline*
and biographies for children

This book is a wonderful gift to Christian families. It is clear, easy to use, and filled with life-changing truths. For parents who want to begin family worship, this is an excellent place to start. For those who want to continue to foster their children's knowledge of the truth through familiarity with the Shorter Catechism, this will be a valuable aid. I will be highly recommending this book to churches and to parents — especially those who are convinced of the importance of raising up the next generation in the knowledge of God and His Word.

JONATHAN L. MASTER
President, Greenville Presbyterian Theological Seminary

Dr. Cathcart's manuscript is outstanding. It will be extremely useful for family and small group teaching/devotions, I highly recommend it. He believes, and strives to live out these truths.

"UNCLE ARCHIE" AKA ARCHIE MOORE,
Chaplain, Ridge Haven, camp, conference and retreat Center

SHORTER CATECHISM DEVOTIONS
TIMELESS TRUTHS FOR TODAY
ROBERT D. CATHCART

CF4KIDS

To my five children,
eight nieces, and four nephews:
May you forever glorify and enjoy Him!

Copyright © Christian Focus Publications 2025

Hardback ISBN: 978-1-5271-1251-3
Ebook ISBN: 978-1-5271-1291-9

10 9 8 7 6 5 4 3 2 1

First published in 2025
in the CF4K imprint
by
Christian Focus Publications Ltd,
Geanies House, Fearn, Ross-shire,
IV20 1TW, Great Britain

www.christianfocus.com

Cover design by Alister MacInnes
Typeset by Pete Barnsley (CreativeHoot.com)

Printed by Bell & Bain

MIX
Paper | Supporting responsible forestry
FSC
www.fsc.org
FSC® C007785

1

SHORTER CATECHISM
QUESTION 1

Q1 | WHAT IS THE CHIEF END OF MAN?

A. Man's chief end is to glorify God, and to enjoy Him forever.

EXPLANATION:

A window's primary purpose is to let in light. A piano's primary purpose is to make music. A treadmill's primary purpose is for exercise (even though the one in my house became a coat rack!). God's Word tells us that our primary purpose – both now and forever – is to glorify God and to enjoy Him. That's why He made us!

So, what does it mean to glorify God here on the earth? It means to reflect His image, His character, His truth, goodness, and beauty (Philippians 4:8). It means to worship Him alone and "to have no other gods before Him" (Exodus 20:3). It means to "seek first His kingdom and His righteousness" (Matthew 6:33). It means to honor and obey His Word

(1 Samuel 15:24; John 14:15). This is what we are to do 24/7, whether we're at home, at school, or at work:

> "So, whether you eat or drink, or whatever you do, do all to the glory of God" (1 Corinthians 10:31).

So, what does it mean to enjoy God here on the earth? It means delighting in our relationship with the Triune God, "spending time reading and meditating on His Word, singing His praise, and speaking to Him in prayer. It means rejoicing in all the blessings we're given by our Heavenly Father (James 1:17), by His Son (Ephesians 1:3ff), and by His Spirit (Galatians 5:22). We can even "count it all joy when we meet trials of various kinds" (James 1:3,4) because we know that God is at work in our lives for our good and for His glory. That's why Paul tells us:

> "Rejoice in the Lord always; again, I will say, rejoice" (Philippians 4:4).

And the best news is this – we'll be *glorifying* God forever, as we sing with the saints and the angels:

> "Worthy are you, our Lord and God, to receive glory and honor and power, for you created all things, and by your will they existed and were created" (Revelation 4:11).

And as we're glorifying Him, we'll also be *enjoying* Him forever, as David proclaims:

> "You make known to me the path of life; in your presence there is fullness of joy; at your right hand are pleasures forevermore" (Psalm 16:11).

CHALLENGE QUESTIONS:

- How can we glorify God today?
- How can we enjoy Him?
- When is it easy to have joy in the Lord?
- When is it harder?

PRAYER

"Not to us, O LORD, not to us, but to your name give glory, for the sake of your steadfast love and your faithfulness" (Psalm 115:1). Help us, heavenly Father, to shine the light of Jesus Christ to everyone we meet and in everything that we do, so that they "may see your good works and give glory to your Father who is in heaven" (Matthew 5:16). May the joy of the LORD be our strength (Nehemiah 8:10) as we serve you and our neighbors. In Jesus' name, Amen.

SHORTER CATECHISM
QUESTION 2

Q2 | WHAT RULE HATH GOD GIVEN TO DIRECT US HOW WE MAY GLORIFY AND ENJOY HIM?

A.   The Word of God, which is contained in the Scriptures of the Old and New Testaments, is the only rule to direct us how we may glorify and enjoy him.

EXPLANATION:

Imagine that a friend has invited you to a big party in a very remote location. How would you feel if this friend gave you an address but didn't provide directions to get there? The location is so remote that GPS doesn't work. That would be frustrating, wouldn't it? You know the goal, the destination, but you don't know how to get there! Thankfully, our Lord isn't like that. Not only does He give us the destination (our chief end or "primary purpose"), He also provides very specific directions! God's Word is "a lamp to our feet and a light to our path" (Psalm 119:105).

Yes! God Himself speaks to us in the Bible, both in the Old and New Testaments, all 66 books! The whole Bible (Genesis-Revelation) is His *only* rule, His *only* standard, His *only* authority over every part of our lives. Paul says it this way:

> "All Scripture is breathed out by God and profitable for teaching, for reproof, for correction, and for training in righteousness, that the man of God may be complete, equipped for every good work" (2 Timothy 3:16-17).

God has given us everything we need to glorify and enjoy Him in the Scriptures, all things that "pertain to life and godliness" (2 Peter 1:3). That doesn't mean we shouldn't read good Christian books or even study this catechism, but these are only helpful when they're true to what the Bible teaches. And since God's Holy Spirit inspired the biblical authors, you can trust every word. There's no "fake news" in the Bible like we often see on Facebook, Twitter, Instagram, or from our crazy relatives! As David writes:

> "The words of the LORD are pure words, like silver refined in a furnace on the ground, purified seven times" (Psalm 12:6).

Also, God's Word never fails. If God says it, He will do it. Sometimes, we don't keep our word because we forget, or because we're lazy, or because we simply change our minds. But listen to what God tells us through the prophet Isaiah:

> "The grass withers, the flower fades, but the word of our God will stand forever" (Isaiah 40:8).

> "So shall my word be that goes out from my mouth; it shall not return to me empty, but it shall accomplish that which I purpose, and shall succeed in the thing for which I sent it" (Isaiah 55:11).

Think of it! We have God's trustworthy (authoritative), spoken (inspired), perfect (inerrant), never-failing (infallible) Word as our map. But we won't reach our goal of glorifying and enjoying Him if we don't read it!

CHALLENGE QUESTIONS:

- What's your favorite Bible Story and why?

- How often do you read the Bible on your own?

- What big questions do you have when you read it?

PRAYER:

Heavenly Father, help us to read, delight in, and meditate on your Word so that we're like trees planted by streams of water, bearing fruit in season, and having no fear of withering leaves. May all that we do in your name prosper (Psalm 1:3). These things we ask in Jesus' name, Amen.

SHORTER CATECHISM
QUESTION 3

Q3 | WHAT DO THE SCRIPTURES PRINCIPALLY TEACH?

A. The Scriptures principally teach what man is to believe concerning God, and what duty God requires of man.

EXPLANATION:

Each summer, before students head off to college, they spend a day or so on campus at orientation. Orientation is when they get to know the campus, register for classes, buy books, meet roommates, and most importantly, find the cafeteria! The answer to this question is our orientation to the Bible. It helps us figure out what to look for when we're reading. The catechism tells us that there are two big ideas to look for in the Bible.

First, the Scriptures teach what we're to believe about God. Over the next few weeks, we're going to see that our God is Creator (Genesis 1, 2), Provider (Psalm 104:10-18), and Redeemer (Hebrews 9:12). We'll learn that there is only one God (Deuteronomy 6:4) and that He exists as a Trinity of Persons; Father, Son, and Holy Spirit (Matthew 28:19). In the next devotion, we'll get to know even more about His amazing character! Here's a sneak-peek:

> "The LORD, the LORD, a God merciful and gracious, slow to anger, and abounding in steadfast love and faithfulness, keeping steadfast love for thousands, forgiving iniquity and transgression and sin, but who will by no means clear the guilty, visiting the iniquity of the fathers on the children and the children's children, to the third and the fourth generation" (Exodus 34:6-7).

For the Christian, the more we get to know about God, the more we grow in our belief in Him, in our faith and trust. This is especially true as we learn about the love of Jesus, who died on the cross for our sins. We read in Luke 24 that the whole Old Testament teaches us "that the Christ should suffer and on the third day rise from the dead," (Luke 24:46-47), the very thing we must believe in order to be saved!

The Scriptures also teach what duty God requires of us. Since God is Creator, Provider, and Redeemer, we should live as thankful, obedient, loving children. Toward the end of the catechism, we'll take a close look at the ten commandments (Exodus 20:1-17; Deuteronomy 5:6-21). The Bible teaches that if we obey what God commands, He will bless us (Deuteronomy 30:16)! Our Lord Jesus sums up His commandments for us:

> "You shall love the Lord your God with all your heart and with all your soul and with all your strength and

with all your mind, and your neighbor as yourself" (Luke 10:27).

Yes! When we love God and neighbor, we keep His commandments. Remember the words of Jesus:

"If you love Me, you will keep My commandments" (John 14:15).

As you hear sermons, Sunday School lessons, and search the Scriptures on your own, seek to know God through His Word so that you know what you believe and how you should live for His glory.

CHALLENGE QUESTIONS:

How would you summarize the story of the Bible?

- Does obeying God's Word save us? (Galatians 2:16)

- Why should we obey the law (James 2:17-18)?

PRAYER:

Dear Heavenly Father, help us to love your Word, to search it like we're looking for the finest gold. May it be sweeter to our taste than honey (Psalm 19:10). As we read the Bible, may we "trust and obey, for there's no other way to be happy in Jesus but to trust and obey."[1] In Jesus' name we pray, Amen.

---

1   John H. Stammis, "Trust and Obey."

4

SHORTER CATECHISM
QUESTION 4

Q4 | WHAT IS GOD?

A. God is a Spirit, infinite, eternal, and unchangeable in His being, wisdom, power, holiness, justice, goodness, and truth.

EXPLANATION:

Have you ever looked up the meaning of an unfamiliar word online or in a dictionary? Some people have a hard time defining God and they try to do it apart from the Bible. Now, we know that words can't truly express all of His fullness, all of His wonder, all of His majesty. But God's Word tells us so much about Him. It tells us that He is different from the rest of His creation. He is even distinct from the people that He made to reflect His image. Though we share many characteristics with our Creator, He is distinguished from us. As Jesus proclaims, "God is spirit" (John 4:24).

Yes. We, too, have a spirit or a soul, but we also have bodies. The Bible does speak about God's eyes (Genesis 6:8), ears (Psalm 130:2), hands (Deuteronomy 5:15), arms (Deuteronomy 33:27), feet (Exodus 24:10), mouth (Isaiah 40), and even His heart (1 Samuel 13:14). But this is His way of helping us understand that He sees, hears, works, speaks, and loves.

We also read that God is infinite, meaning that He cannot be contained in time or space.[2] He is everywhere! He fills the heavens and the earth (1 Kings 8:27). He's also eternal, without beginning or end!

"Before the mountains were brought forth, or ever you had formed the earth and the world, from everlasting to everlasting you are God" (Psalm 90:2).

God is also unchangeable. He's the same "yesterday, today, and forever" (Hebrew 13:18). As James writes, with God, "... there is no variation or shadow due to change" (James 1:27).

How marvelous is our God! Everything about Him, His whole being is infinite, eternal, and unchangeable! This includes:

His wisdom, because there's nothing that He doesn't see, know, or understand (Psalm 139:1-12).

His power, because He can do all things, including creating and upholding the universe (Romans 1:20).

His holiness, because He's set apart from His creation and is perfect in every way (Isaiah 6:3).

---

2   Thomas Vincent, *The Shorter Catechism Explained from Scripture* (The Banner of Truth Trust: 3 Murrayfield R., Edinburgh) 1980, p. 27.

His justice, because everything He says and does is right (Psalm 119:128).

His goodness, because He is the source of all good[3] (James 1:17).

His truth, because He always speaks the truth and it is impossible for Him to lie (Hebrews 6:18).

What an incredible definition of God the catechism gives us! I hope that you'll memorize it so that you grow to know, love, and worship Him even more.

CHALLENGE QUESTIONS:

- What are some things that people often get wrong about God?
- What is the danger of defining God apart from the Bible?
- How does our being, wisdom, power, holiness, justice, goodness, and truth differ from God's?

PRAYER:

"To the King of the ages, immortal, invisible, the only God, be honor and glory forever and ever" (1 Timothy 1:17). Father, Son, and Holy Spirit may we magnify and exalt your Holy name in all that we say, think, feel, and do. In Jesus' name, Amen.

---

3   Ibid, p.33.

5

SHORTER CATECHISM
QUESTION 5

Q5 | ARE THERE MORE GODS THAN ONE?

A. There is but one only, the living and true God.

EXPLANATION:

"Should I choose a cheeseburger, chicken nuggets, fish sandwich or something healthier, like a fresh wrap or a salad?" Have you ever had a hard time choosing something to eat at a restaurant? Menus can be overwhelming, whether we're holding them in our hands or quickly scanning the digital drive-thru ones. Some people think choosing a god to worship is like that. It seems like there are many good options, but they don't know which one to pick. However, the Bible is clear. There is only one God, and He alone is to be worshiped!

Did you know that every Israelite girl and boy memorized these words and recited them every day?

"Hear, O Israel: The LORD our God, the LORD is one" (Deuteronomy 6:4).

You see, all the other gods that people worship are idols, false gods. The Bible says this about them:

"Their idols are silver and gold, the work of human hands. They have mouths, but do not speak; eyes, but do not see. They have ears, but do not hear; noses, but do not smell. They have hands, but do not feel; feet, but do not walk; and they do not make a sound in their throat" (Psalm 115:4-7).

These false gods are mute, blind, and deaf. They can't feel, walk, or speak. This is true of statues, carvings, and drawings, but also the idols we worship in our hearts like social media popularity, education, or body image.

But our God is the Great I AM (Exodus 3:14), who has always lived, is living now, and will always live. He's the One who gives life to all His creation, including you and me: "For in Him we live and move, and have our being" (Acts 17:28).

Our God is also the only One who gives us spiritual life. The Holy Spirit, who breathed life into Adam causes us to be born again (John 3:8). We know that our Lord Jesus Christ is the Resurrection and the Life (John 11) who raised Lazarus from the dead. He is the Way, the Truth, and the Life and if we believe in Him, we will live with Him forever in His Father's house (John 14:1-6).

What a difference between the one, true, living God, and all false, dead idols. When we worship them, we become like them (Psalm 115:8). Instead of being vibrant and full of life, we become dull and lifeless as they make us their slaves. But when we trust in and worship the one true God through Jesus Christ His Son, the Holy Spirit fills us with living water and abundant life. And unlike all false religions, salvation doesn't come through what we do for "god" but through what our gracious God has done for us.

So the choice isn't that hard after all, is it?

"Worship the LORD in the splendor of holiness; tremble before him, all the earth (Psalm 96:9)" for He alone is the one, true, and living God (1 Thessalonians 1:9)!

CHALLENGE QUESTIONS:

- What would you say to someone who says: "All roads lead to heaven so why does it matter which god I choose?"

- Can you name some modern-day idols that take your attention away from God?

PRAYER:

Heavenly Father, may we have no gods before you and may we love you with heart, soul, mind, and strength. Forgive us when we've worshiped idols. Help us to turn away from our sins and to turn our eyes upon Jesus. In His name we pray, Amen.

6

SHORTER CATECHISM
QUESTION 6

Q.6 | HOW MANY PERSONS ARE THERE IN THE GODHEAD?

A. There are three persons in the Godhead; the Father, the Son, and the Holy Spirit, and these three are one God, the same in substance, equal in power and glory.

EXPLANATION:

How can God be three-in-one? In many ways it is mysterious and there are things about God that are past our figuring out, but that shouldn't surprise or worry us. As the Lord declares, "my thoughts are not your thoughts, neither are your ways my ways....For as the heavens are higher than the earth, so are my ways higher than your ways and my thoughts than your thoughts" (Isaiah 55:8-9). Over the last 2,000 years, lots of people have tried to explain the mystery of the Trinity and some of those explanations have hurt rather than helped us understand our God. But the Bible has much to say about the Father, Son, and the Holy Spirit!

First, we know that there are three Persons in the Godhead, which is a word that means God's nature or essence.[4] All three of these Persons are of the same substance; they're all truly God. As early as the first chapter of Genesis, we hear: "And God said, 'Let *us* make man in *our* image, after *our* likeness" (Genesis 1:26). And One Person is not "better" than any of the other three, neither is one Person stronger or more praiseworthy. All three are "equal in power and glory." All three are worthy to be worshiped and praised! This is the testimony of Scripture.

> Consider the Father: "Blessed be the God and Father of our Lord Jesus Christ" (Ephesians 1:3).

Consider the Son: "...and his name shall be called Wonderful Counselor, *Mighty God*, Everlasting Father, Prince of Peace" (Isaiah 9:6). The Apostle John adds: "And the Word (the Son) became flesh and dwelt among us, and we have seen His glory, glory as of the only Son from the Father, full of grace and truth" (John 1:14).

Consider the Holy Spirit: When Ananias lied about what he and his wife, Saphira, gave to the church, Peter challenges him by asking, "Ananias, why has Satan filled your heart to lie to the *Holy Spirit* ....You have not lied to man but *to God*" (Acts 5:3-4).

It is also clear that the three persons of the Trinity are individual and distinct, not just one Person playing three different parts. Consider this scene from Jesus' baptism, where all three Persons are present together and are doing three distinct, but

---

4   Thomas Boston, *An Exposition of the Assembly's Shorter Catechism*, Common Domain.

united things: "And when *Jesus* was baptized, immediately He went up from the water, and behold, the heavens were opened to Him, and He saw the *Spirit of God* descending like a dove and coming to rest on Him, and behold, a *voice from heaven* said, 'This is *My beloved Son*, with whom I am well pleased" (Matthew 3: 16-17).

As we walk through the rest of the catechism, we'll get to see the wonderful work of each Person of the Trinity. As we do so, may we grow in our love for and devotion to the One, Triune God.

CHALLENGE QUESTIONS:

- How would you answer someone who says the Trinity is not mentioned in the Bible?

- Why do Christians believe that God exists in three Persons?

- Name some things we see the Father, Son, and Holy Spirit doing in Scripture that prove each Person is truly God.

PRAYER:

"May the grace of the Lord Jesus Christ and the love of God and the fellowship of the Holy Spirit be with all of us today" (I1 Corinthians 13:14) as we seek to grow in our knowledge and understanding of who you are, O God. In Jesus' name we pray, Amen.

SHORTER CATECHISM
QUESTION 7

Q7 | WHAT ARE THE DECREES OF GOD?

A. The decrees of God are His eternal purpose, according to the counsel of His will, whereby, for His own glory, He hath foreordained whatsoever comes to pass.

EXPLANATION:

When we hear the word "decree", we probably think about a king or a ruler who orders his people to carry out his plan. Well, that's exactly what the catechism is teaching us! Our King, the Triune God, has decreed His plan, His blueprint[5] for whatever has happened in the past, is happening now, and will happen forever. As we read in Ephesians:

"He works all things according to the counsel of his will." (Ephesians 1:11).

---

5   GI Williamson, *The Westminster Shorter Catechism for Study Classes* (Presbyterian and Reformed Publishing: Phillipsburg, NJ), 2003, p. 28.

And the difference between God's plan and any we might make – even the plans of kings and queens – is that His plan stands forever. If we're building a house, we might draw the blueprints ahead of time, but then decide, "we need a bigger closet here" or "let's add a 60-inch flat screen to the man cave." We might carefully plan our day down to the last minute, only to have our agenda overturned by an emergency or some other surprise. But God's plan never changes because, as we learned, He is infinite, eternal, and unchangeable. Nothing surprises Him because He knows all things, and nothing can stop Him because He is all-powerful. As the LORD Himself testifies:

> "For I am God, and there is no other; I am God, and there is none like me, declaring the end from the beginning and from ancient times things not yet done, saying, 'My counsel shall stand, and I will accomplish all my purpose... I have spoken, and I will bring it to pass; I have purposed, and I will do it" (Isaiah 46:9-11).

Maybe you've heard parents, or older Christians say that God is sovereign. This means that He's in control of everything that happens, whether good things or bad things. This may seem hard to understand, but we have this precious promise:

> "And we know that for those who love God *all things* (good and bad) work together for good, for those who are called according to his purpose" (Romans 8:28).

Sometimes, life is hard. People get sick. Accidents happen. Loved ones die. We're not treated fairly. We miss the big shot, crack the high note, fail the test. But even these things are planned by God for our good and for His glory!

Do you remember the story of Joseph and his brothers? They seized him, ripped off his coat, threw him into a pit, and then sold him into slavery. Talk about a hard life! But what did he say when he held all the power in Egypt years later, not only to help the people in famine, but also to take revenge on his brothers?

"Do not fear, for am I in the place of God? As for you, you meant evil against me, but God meant it for good, to bring it about that many people should be kept alive, as they are today" (Genesis 50:19-20).

CHALLENGE QUESTIONS:

- Think about a time when you or your family had to change plans.

- Why is it comforting to know that God's plan for you never changes?

PRAYER:

King Jesus, you are the Alpha and the Omega (the first and the last), the beginning and the end (Revelation 21:6). May we put our trust in you, even when times are hard, knowing that everything works together for our good. In Jesus' name, Amen.

SHORTER CATECHISM
QUESTIONS 8 & 9

Q8 | HOW DOTH GOD EXECUTE HIS DECREES?

A. God executeth His decrees in the works of creation and providence.

EXPLANATION:

Yesterday, we looked at God's powerful, eternal plan for all things. This answer tells us how He executes or carries out His plan: through His works of creation and providence. Today, we'll begin to examine His work of creation. Later we will look at His work of providence in Q.11.

Q9 | WHAT IS THE WORK OF CREATION?

A. The work of creation is God's making all things of nothing, by the word of His power, in the space of six days, and all very good.

EXPLANATION:

Do you remember playing with Lego bricks or similar construction toys? My boys used to save up for the latest sets. Some days, they would take colorful bricks from previous builds and come up with imaginative, beautiful, and detailed creations. Well, what our God does in creation is even better!

When we attempt to "create" or build something, we gather the necessary supplies like wood, hammers, nails, or paint. Or we may simply empty them out of a box (like Legos) and follow the instructions. But God makes all things out of nothing!

"In the beginning God created the heavens and the earth" (Genesis 1:1).

He even makes the building blocks, even the tiniest things we can't see like soundwaves, atoms, and the human cell. The author of Hebrews says it this way:

"By faith we understand that the universe was created by the word of God, so that what is seen was not made out of things that are visible" (Hebrews 11:3).

And God is so powerful that He makes all things out of nothing by simply speaking:

"By the word of the LORD the heavens were made, and by the breath of his mouth all their host...For he spoke, and it came to be; he commanded, and it stood firm" (Psalm 33:6, 9).

Not only does He speak all things into existence, He finished in six short days (Genesis 1:3-28)! And unlike our faulty or flawed "creations," everything God made was good:

"And God saw everything that he had made, and behold, it was very good" (Genesis 1:31).

Now, be aware that there are many who don't understand or believe that God created the world in this wonderful way. Some teach a random "big bang" created the universe, but they can't explain who/what caused it or where the basic building blocks for life came from. Others teach that "the cosmos (universe) is all that is or was or ever will be."[6] But rest assured that "the heavens declare the glory of God, and the sky above proclaims His handiwork" (Psalm 19:1). The design, beauty, and purpose of creation testifies that the Triune God personally made the heavens and the earth and everything in them, including you and me!

CHALLENGE QUESTIONS:

- Go outside and look around. How does God's creation testify that He created the world (Psalm 19:1-6)?

- What would you say to someone who insists that God couldn't have created the world in only six days?

PRAYER:

We thank you, Father, for creating this beautiful world. May we point others to you as we see your glory reflected in creation. In Jesus' name we pray, Amen.

---

6   Carl Sagan, *Cosmos* (Ballantine Books: New York, 1980), p. 1.

SHORTER CATECHISM
QUESTION 10

Q10 | HOW DID GOD CREATE MAN?

A. God created man, male and female, after His own image, in knowledge, righteousness, and holiness, with dominion over the creatures.

EXPLANATION:

Earlier, we talked about how God made all things, including the heavens and the earth and everything in them, by the word of His power, simply by speaking them into existence. There is one exception – the creation of Adam and Eve. This He did personally!

"The LORD God formed the man of dust from the ground and breathed into his nostrils the breath of life, and the man became a living creature... So the LORD God caused a deep sleep to fall upon the man, and while he slept took one of his ribs and closed up its place with flesh. And the rib that the LORD God had taken from the man he made into a woman and brought her to the man" (Genesis 2:7, 21-22).

You see, God created Adam and Eve different from the rest of His creation, even the most magnificent animals, because we are made in His image. This means that we have living souls that are like Him in "knowledge, righteousness, and holiness." Knowledge means that our minds can think, know God, and understand His Word. Righteousness means that we know right from wrong. Holiness means that we are set apart from the rest of creation to have a special relationship with God. Because of this, every human life is special from the moment a baby is conceived until the time of death. So we must treat all people with dignity and respect.

God also specially created Adam as man and Eve as woman to form a special partnership we call marriage, to live together as "one flesh" (Genesis 2:24-25). Yes. Adam and Eve are our first parents. And the Lord commissions them:

> "Be fruitful and multiply and fill the earth and subdue it, and have dominion over the fish of the sea and over the birds of the heavens and over every living thing that moves on the earth" (Genesis 1:28).

Men and women are to carry out God's commission to have families, to cultivate the earth, and to take care of His creation. He gives Adam and all men specific duties; men are to "work and keep" (Genesis 2:15). Likewise, Eve and all women after her enjoy a special calling to be helpers. They're to enable, encourage, and work alongside their husbands to fulfill what God has called them both to do (Genesis 2:18).

Denying these truths about men and women, as many in our culture do today, is rebellion against the Lord's beautiful design and only ends in frustration, defeat, and death, if there is no repentance. Embracing these truths brings the Lord's blessing. Men and women – whether married or single – work together to bring glory to His name. Christian marriages are also a beautiful picture of Christ's love for the church whom He bought with His own blood.

Let's pray that God will raise up young men and women who embrace His loving design and calling for their lives, and who treat all of those made in His image with dignity and respect. What a testimony they would be to our world!

CHALLENGE QUESTIONS:

- Why should we treat all people respectfully, even if we disagree with them?

- What are some ways that young men can grow in their calling "to work and to keep?"

- What are some ways young women can grow into capable helpers in God's kingdom?

- How can we all be more productive as we subdue the earth for Christ?

PRAYER:

Gracious Heavenly Father, we thank you that we are "fearfully and wonderfully made" (Psalm 139:13-15). We are made in your image! Help us to grow in our knowledge of you, our righteousness as we follow your Son, and our holiness as you restore your perfect image in us by your Spirit. In Jesus' name we pray, Amen.

11

SHORTER CATECHISM
QUESTION 11

Q11 | WHAT ARE GOD'S WORKS OF PROVIDENCE?

A. God's works of providence are His most holy, wise, and powerful preserving and governing all His creatures, and all their actions.

EXPLANATION:

Recently, I watched a video of a mother duck walking along the road with her babies. It's always fun to see how these cuddly creatures follow their mother in a straight line, especially knowing how hard it is to get little boys and girls to do the same! This time, though, a crow appeared, hoping to snack on one of the ducklings. The mother duck wasn't having it! She hid those ducklings under her wings, fended off the stealthy attacks of the crow, and led her brood to the safety of some nearby underbrush. In some small way, this mother duck illustrates God's marvelous works of providence as He "powerfully preserves and governs all His creatures and all their actions."

Think of the way that God preserves (takes care of, protects, provides for) all His creation by His powerful hand. The Bible tells us that Christ Himself, "upholds the universe by the word of His power (Hebrews 1:3) ....in Him all things hold together (Colossians 1:17). If He let go, the whole universe would fall apart!

Our God is also personally involved in preserving every one of His creatures, down to the last detail. He posts boundaries for the seas, provides springs of water and food for the animals, grows trees for birds to nest in, and oversees the rising and setting of the sun to mark time for work and rest (Psalm 104:5-26). As the Psalmist writes:

> "When you give it to them, they gather it up; when you open your hand, they are filled with good things. When you hide Your face, they are dismayed; when you take away their breath, they die and return to their dust" (Psalm 104:27-29).

Not only does our Lord preserve, He also governs (orders, directs) what His creatures do, including you and me! As Solomon tells us, "The heart of man plans his way, but the LORD establishes his steps" (Proverbs 16:9). This is true even for the mightiest king, president, or world leader:

> "The king's heart is a stream of water in the hand of the LORD; he turns it wherever he will" (Proverbs 21:1).

In our Lord's wisdom and goodness, He has "written in His book, every one of them, the days that were formed for us, when as yet there was none of them" (Psalm 139:16).

How comforting to know that through His works of providence, the Lord keeps our very lives, "our going out and our coming in from this time forth and forevermore" (Psalm 121:5-8). And we can trust that His preserving and governing is always for the good of His children (Romans 8:28) because "the LORD is righteous in all His ways and kind in all His works" (Psalm 145:17). Even more, unlike even the most attentive mother duck, nothing can harm us unless our God allows it. As the Heidelberg Catechism reminds us, "Without the will of my Father in heaven not a hair can fall from my head!"[7]

CHALLENGE QUESTIONS:

- What does it mean that God preserves us?

- What does it mean that He governs our actions?

- How does God use even the sinful actions of people for His glory and our good (Acts 2:22-24)?

PRAYER:

Heavenly Father, you keep us as the apple of your eye; you hide us under the shadow of your wings (Psalm 17:8). Thank you for providing our daily bread, protecting us from evil, and directing our steps each day. In Jesus' name, Amen.

---

7 *The Heidelberg Catechism* (The Banner of Truth Trust: 3 Murrayfield R., Edinburgh, 2013), p.9.

SHORTER CATECHISM
QUESTION 12

Q12 | WHAT SPECIAL ACT OF PROVIDENCE DID GOD EXERCISE TOWARD MAN IN THE ESTATE WHEREIN HE WAS CREATED?

A.   When God had created man, He entered into a covenant of life with him, upon condition of perfect obedience; forbidding him to eat of the tree of the knowledge of good and evil, upon the pain of death.

EXPLANATION:

Think about all of the wonderful blessings God gave Adam in the Garden of Eden:

- A perfect paradise to cultivate and explore
- A plentiful supply of food and water
- A wide variety of animals to observe and watch over
- A wife to share his life with and to help him
- A day of rest to enjoy God's good creation

Yet, the best was still to come! God makes a covenant or agreement with Adam, promising him natural, spiritual, and eternal life[8] if he would obey His Word not to eat from a certain tree:

> "And the LORD God commanded the man, saying, "You may surely eat of every tree of the garden, but of the tree of the knowledge of good and evil you shall not eat, for in the day that you eat of it you shall surely die" (Genesis 2:16-17).

Often, this special agreement is called "the covenant of works" because God's promise of life depends on whether Adam obeys or not. Now, at this point, Adam and Eve weren't exactly like you and me. They were without sin. They had the power to freely choose between good or evil, to obey or disobey, to live or die. They also enjoyed all the blessings of Eden, including the Tree of Life, as proof of God's goodness to them. We'll talk about Adam's tragic choice in the weeks to come that brought upon us all "the wages of sin" (Romans 6:23), which is natural, spiritual, and eternal death.[9]

But we can always be thankful that God Himself desires to have a special relationship with us. He makes promises to us that He always keeps, even though it would cost Him the death of His Son (see Romans 5:6-21). And let us never forget that He sets the terms of our relationship with Him because He is our Creator King.

---

8   Thomas Vincent, *The Shorter Catechism Explained from Scripture* (The Banner of Truth Trust: 3 Murrayfield R., Edinburgh) 1980, p. 52.

9   Ibid, p. 53

CHALLENGE QUESTIONS:

- Describe some of the blessings that Adam and Eve enjoyed in the Garden of Eden. Before the fall, how were Adam and Eve like us?

- How were they different?

- How is God's covenant with Adam a "covenant of life?" How is God's covenant with Adam a "covenant of works?"

PRAYER:

Heavenly Father, You made us; we are Yours. We are Your people, the sheep of Your pasture (Psalm 100:3). Thank You for creating us to be Your loving children. Give us hearts to love, obey, and live for Your glory. In Jesus' name we pray, Amen.

SHORTER CATECHISM
QUESTIONS 13-15

Q13 | DID OUR FIRST PARENTS CONTINUE IN THE ESTATE WHEREIN THEY WERE CREATED?

A.   Our first parents, being left to the freedom of their own will, fell from the estate wherein they were created, by sinning against God.

Q15 | WHAT WAS THE SIN WHEREBY OUR FIRST PARENTS FELL FROM THE ESTATE WHEREIN THEY WERE CREATED?

A.   The sin whereby our first parents fell from the estate wherein they were created, was their eating the forbidden fruit.

EXPLANATION:

Has anyone ever come up to you and announced: "I've got good news and I've got bad news? Which do you want first?"

I almost always ask for the bad news first because it makes the good news all the sweeter! In this section of the catechism, we learn the bad news about mankind so that we're prepared to hear the good news of our salvation. Just like a good doctor, Scripture diagnoses our disease (sin) before prescribing the cure (the gospel of Jesus Christ).

From Genesis 3:1-6, we read the serpent's cunning temptation of Eve. She, then, in the freedom of her will, sinned against God by choosing to eat the forbidden fruit. Then, "she....gave some to her husband who was with her, and he ate" (Genesis 3:6). Adam, instead of obeying God and choosing the life that He promised, sinned against Him and broke the covenant of life. Then "the eyes of both were opened, and they knew that they were naked" (Genesis 3:7). Instead of being more "like God" as Satan falsely promised, they suddenly realized how unlike Him they had become by their sin, and they try their best to hide from His holiness.

But exactly what is sin?

Q14 | WHAT IS SIN?

A.   **Sin is any want of conformity unto, or transgression of the law of God.**

EXPLANATION:

No question. There are some big words in that definition of sin. But it boils down to two ideas:

Want of conformity means, "not being or doing what God requires"[10] in His Word. It's like when your mother tells you to clean your room, practice the piano, or wash your hands before supper and you simply don't do it! In the Bible, it's like the prophet Jonah refusing to go to Nineveh even though God plainly tells him to do it. You may have heard adults call these sins of omission.

Transgression of the law of God is like when you see a "Do Not Enter" sign and you go in anyway. This is what Adam and Eve did by eating from the tree of the knowledge of good and evil, even after God graciously told them not to do it. You may have heard adults call these sins of commission.

Both sins of omission and commission are rebellion against our holy, loving, heavenly Father, and are equally deserving of eternal death. Thankfully, He has made a way for us to be forgiven from all our sins.

CHALLENGE QUESTIONS:

- What lies did Satan tell Eve (Genesis 3:1-6)?
- What kinds of lies does he use to tempt us today?

---

10 *Catechism for Young Children Original Edition: An Introduction to the Shorter Catechism* (Christian Education and Publications, Lawrenceville, GA), p.4. https://www.pcabookstore.com/p-79-catechism-for-young-children-original-edition.aspx

PRAYER:

Heavenly Father, "we have left undone those things which we ought to have done, and we have done those things which we ought not to have done" (Book of Common Prayer). Please forgive us, as You forgave our first parents. Through the blood of Jesus, we pray. Amen.

SHORTER CATECHISM
QUESTIONS 16 & 17

Q16 | DID ALL MANKIND FALL IN ADAM'S FIRST TRANSGRESSION?

A. The covenant being made with Adam, not only for himself, but for his posterity; all mankind, descending from him by ordinary generation, sinned in him, and fell with him, in his first transgression.

EXPLANATION:

Have you ever been part of electing someone to serve in an office? Maybe you're too young to vote for president, Prime Minister, senator, governor, or mayor, but perhaps you've participated in class or club elections. What do we elect these people to do? To represent us. We can't all crowd into the White House, or Houses of Parliament, but our elected officials represent us and act on our behalf. Well, this is what Adam did for us in the covenant of life (or works). He was our God-appointed representative. So, when Adam sinned by eating the forbidden fruit, all mankind – with one exception (our Lord Jesus Christ) – sinned in him. This is the clear teaching of Scripture:

"Therefore...sin came into the world through one man, and death through sin, and so death spread to all men because all sinned" (Romans 5:12).

The Catechism explains just how far we've fallen in Adam:

Q17 | INTO WHAT ESTATE DID THE FALL BRING MANKIND?

A. The fall brought mankind into an estate of sin and misery.

EXPLANATION:

We'll study more about our fallen condition in the next couple of days. Yet, there is hope because there is One who was not born "by ordinary generation," that is, not by an earthly father:

"Now the birth of Jesus Christ took place in this way. When his mother Mary had been betrothed to Joseph, before they came together she was found to be with child from the Holy Spirit" (Matthew 1:18).

And He alone is the representative who saves us from our sins:

"For as in Adam all die, so also in Christ shall all be made alive" (1 Corinthians 15:22).

One thing to note: It is popular, sometimes even among some "smart people" who claim the name of Jesus, to say that Adam was not a true, historical person. Instead of agreeing with Scripture's account that Adam was specially created by God out of the dust of the ground (Genesis 2:7), they say that humans evolved over millions of years. And a story about an enchanted garden, a talking serpent, and a forbidden tree is the stuff of myths. It's a fable to teach right from wrong and to be on guard against temptation. The problem is this – If Adam and Eve aren't historical people, if they didn't truly eat from the tree of the knowledge of good and evil, plunging us into sin, then the rest of the Bible falls apart. It calls the authority of Paul (see passages above) and Jesus (Matthew 19:4) into question and denies our need for a Savior.

But we know God's Word is true:

> "For there is no distinction: for all have sinned and fall short of the glory of God, and (*all who believe in Him*) are justified by his grace as a gift, through the redemption that is in Christ Jesus" (Romans 3:22-24).

CHALLENGE QUESTIONS:

- What are some of the duties of elected officials in representing us?

- How would you answer someone who says, "It's not fair that when Adam sinned, I sinned? I wasn't even there!" How is Jesus a new and better Adam, a new and better representative?

PRAYER:

Thank you, Heavenly Father, that you sent a second Adam to obey, to suffer, to die, and to rise again so that we might be saved once and for all for our sins (Romans 5:12-21). In His name we pray, Amen.

SHORTER CATECHISM
QUESTION 18

Q18 | WHEREIN CONSISTS THE SINFULNESS OF THAT ESTATE WHEREINTO MAN FELL?

A. The sinfulness of that estate whereinto man fell consists in the guilt of Adam's first sin, the want of original righteousness, and the corruption of his whole nature, which is commonly called Original Sin, together with all actual transgressions which proceed from it.

EXPLANATION:

When you were little, did you ever want to fly? Maybe you climbed high in a tree or looked out on the edge of a cliff and thought "I wish I could be as free as a bird!" Or maybe you crafted a pair of paper wings, ran outside on a breezy day, and started flapping away to see if you'd take flight. We know the results; unlike birds, it's not in our nature to fly.[11] In a similar

---

11 GI Williamson, *The Westminster Shorter Catechism for Study Classes* (Presbyterian and Reformed Publishing: Phillipsburg, NJ), 2003, p. 68.

way, because of Adam's sin, human beings, without God's help, aren't capable of pleasing Him. It's no longer in our nature to love, worship, and obey Him. Let's look at just how far mankind fell in the Garden of Eden.

You may remember from our last devotion that Adam's fall leaves all people (except for Jesus) guilty and no longer in a right relationship with God. As Paul writes:

"For as by the one man's disobedience the many were made sinners (Romans 5:19) ... "None is righteous, no, not one (Romans 3:10).

Therefore, our whole nature is polluted, poisoned, tainted, and corrupted by sin. This includes our minds, wills, words, and actions (Romans 3:10-18). This is what we call original sin, and it touches every part of us. And left to ourselves, we are totally incapable of turning to God for salvation:

"No one seeks for God...There is no fear of God before their eyes" (Romans 3:11, 18).

And not only is there original sin, but there are also actual sins, evil thoughts, words, and actions that flow from our fallen natures. Jesus explains it very well:

"So, every healthy tree bears good fruit, but the diseased tree bears bad fruit. A healthy tree cannot bear bad fruit, nor can a diseased tree bear good fruit" (Matthew 7:17-18)...For out of the heart come evil thoughts, murder, adultery, sexual immorality, theft, false witness, slander" (Matthew 15:19).

But there is good news! The depth of our sin cannot begin to match the depth of God's grace!

"[Though we] were dead in... trespasses and sins...living in the passions of our flesh, carrying out the desires of the body and the mind, and were by nature children of wrath... God, being rich in mercy...made us alive together with Christ—by grace you have been saved" (Ephesians 2:1-5)!

CHALLENGE QUESTIONS:

Read Genesis 6:5 and Jeremiah 17:9.

- How would you respond to someone who says that man is basically good?

- What is the difference between our original sin and our actual sins?

PRAYER:

Our Father, like King David, we confess that we were "brought forth in iniquity" (Psalm 51:5) and that we've sinned against you in our thoughts, words, and actions. Forgive us through the blood of our Lord Jesus, who makes us whole again. In His name we pray, Amen.

19

SHORTER CATECHISM
QUESTION 19

Q19 | WHAT IS THE MISERY OF THAT ESTATE WHEREINTO MEN FELL?

A. All mankind, by their fall, lost communion with God, are under His wrath and curse, and so made liable to all the miseries in this life, to death itself, and to the pains of hell forever.

EXPLANATION:

I know what you're thinking: Wow! How much more bad news can there be? I promise you. Good news is on the way! But there are some truly miserable and awful things we must understand about our fallen condition before we begin to hear the Good News, starting with the next devotion.

First of all, we've lost communion with God. What does this mean? It's very clear in the book of Genesis. Adam and Eve once walked with God "in the cool of the day" and enjoyed His company. But after eating the forbidden fruit, they understood their guilt and shame and tried in vain to "hide themselves from the presence of the LORD God" (Genesis 3:8).

Now, too, instead of enjoying God's favor, they are "by nature children of wrath," (Ephesians 2:3), living under the threat of God's judgment. And instead of enjoying His beautiful blessings – abundant food and water, healthy, pain-free bodies, peaceful relationships, perfect weather, etc. – they are now cursed. And life will become miserable for them:

> "To the woman He said, 'I will surely multiply your pain in childbearing: in pain you shall bring forth children. Your desire shall be for your husband, and he shall rule over you. And to Adam He said... "Cursed is the ground because of you; in pain you shall eat of it all the days of your life; thorns and thistles it shall bring forth for you; and you shall eat of the plants of the field. By the sweat of your face you shall eat bread, till you return to the ground, for out of it you were taken; for you are dust, and to dust you shall return" (Genesis 3:16-19)

Did you hear that last bit? Part of the curse is that Adam and Eve will die, just as the Lord promised they would if they ate the forbidden fruit. They'll return to the ground. Even more, apart from God's grace, they, and all mankind, will spend eternity in hell where there is "weeping and gnashing of teeth" (Matthew 25:30), where "their worm does not die, and the fire is not quenched" (Mark 9:48).

As Paul teaches: "For the wages of sin is death," of body and soul forever. Miserable news, indeed. But thankfully, that's not the end of the story! Paul finishes his thought: "But the free gift of God is eternal life in Christ Jesus our Lord" (Romans 6:23). In the devotions ahead, we'll see how God restores our relationship, satisfies His wrath, reverses the curse, comforts our miseries, and delivers us from death and hell through His Son. And that's good news, indeed!

CHALLENGE QUESTIONS:

- What are some of the miseries of life that we can trace back to the fall?

- What are some ways that people try to hide their guilt and shame from God?

- Read Revelation 21:1-4. When will man and creation finally be restored?

PRAYER:

Gracious Heavenly Father, thank You for the free gift of Your Son who paid for our sins, satisfied Your wrath, and rose again to give us new life. May He comfort us as we go through the miseries of this life and may we look forward to the time when He finishes making all things new. In Jesus' name we pray, Amen.

SHORTER CATECHISM
QUESTION 20

Q20 | DID GOD LEAVE ALL MANKIND TO PERISH IN THE ESTATE OF SIN AND MISERY?

A.   God having, out of his mere good pleasure, from all eternity, elected some to everlasting life, did enter into a covenant of grace, to deliver them out of the estate of sin and misery, and to bring them into an estate of salvation by a Redeemer.

EXPLANATION:

It's about time we had some good news and this answer has lots of it! Even though Adam broke the covenant of works, plunging us into sin and mercy, our good God has promised deliverance for His people. We call this promise the covenant of grace. Paul reveals God's eternal rescue plan in Ephesians 1:

"Blessed be the God and Father of our Lord Jesus Christ, who has blessed us in Christ with every spiritual blessing in the heavenly places, even as he chose us in him before the foundation of the world, that we should be holy and blameless before him. In love he predestined us for adoption to himself as sons through Jesus Christ, according to the purpose of his will" (Eph. 1:3-5).

Yes! Before we had done anything good or bad, God chose or elected us to salvation "out of His mere good pleasure" and so that His "purpose of election might continue" (Rom. 9:11). To be sure, God's choosing us for salvation (and not others) is a mystery and it's hard for us to understand. But remember that, apart from God's mercy, none of us are capable of choosing Him (Romans 3:11-12). If any are to be saved, God, out of mercy, must do the choosing!

Because our God is loving and kind, He announces the covenant of grace to Adam and Eve right after their fall. Our Lord proclaims to Satan, that sly serpent, that he won't win!

"I will put enmity between you and the woman, and between your offspring and her offspring; he shall bruise your head, and you shall bruise his heel" (Genesis 3:15).

As we talked about before, Jesus is our representative. He is the "offspring" or "seed of the woman," our Redeemer. That means He pays the price for our sins through His blood on the cross. Though His heel is bruised (He dies and remains dead for three days), He bruises Satan's head (gives him the deathblow) so that we, His people, are freed from our sins forever! This makes Satan furious and even now he is at war with all of those who are saved by Jesus Christ (Revelation 12:17). But make no mistake! Jesus has won the war through His death and resurrection, even though we still fight battles against Satan today.

You may ask, "How do we connect with God's covenant of grace? When does it become real to us? When do we start to enjoy the benefits and blessings of our salvation?" The answer is by faith. We connect with Jesus when we trust in Jesus Christ alone for our salvation. We'll talk more about faith in the devotions to come, but Paul reminds us that even our faith in Christ is a blessing of God's grace, His unearned and undeserved favor:

> "For by grace you have been saved through faith. And this is not your own doing; it is the gift of God, not a result of works, so that no one may boast" (Ephesians 2:8-9).

Let us thank God that He didn't leave us to die in our sins but chose to deliver us through Jesus, our Redeemer! Let us praise Him for the covenant of grace!

CHALLENGE QUESTIONS:

- When did God plan our salvation from sin?
- How does Jesus redeem us?
- How do we personally connect with the covenant of grace?
- How would you define grace?

PRAYER:

God of grace, thank You for the promise that You are our God and that we are Your people (Jeremiah 11:4). O Lord, we don't deserve Your love, but we are thankful that You have saved us through Jesus Christ our Redeemer. In His gracious name we pray, Amen.

SHORTER CATECHISM
QUESTION 21

Q21 | WHO IS THE REDEEMER OF GOD'S ELECT?

A. The only redeemer of God's elect is the Lord Jesus Christ, who being the eternal Son of God, became man, and so was, and continueth to be, God and man, in two distinct natures, and one person, forever.

EXPLANATION:

You may notice that some of these devotions begin with stories or comparisons that help paint pictures of the truth. However, some truths are so far above our knowledge that our stories or comparisons only hurt our understanding of them. This is true of the Trinity. It's also true about how our Redeemer Jesus Christ is God and man. Thankfully, we're not left in the dark because the Bible tells us so much about Him!

We know that our Redeemer is the eternal Son of God, the Second Person of the Trinity. Here are some of the wonderful things said about Him in the New Testament:

> "In the beginning was the Word, and the Word was with God, and the Word was God" (John 1:1).

> "For by Him all things were created, in heaven and on earth, visible and invisible...all things were created through Him and for Him. And He is before all things" (Colossians 1:16-17).

> "...His Son, whom He appointed heir all of all things....He is the radiance of the glory of God and the exact imprint of His nature, and He upholds the universe by the word of His power" (Hebrews 1:2-3).

That's what makes the covenant of grace so marvelous! God's Son "humbled Himself...by being born in the likeness of men" (Philippians 2:5-8). As Paul writes:

> "But when the fullness of time had come, God sent forth his Son, born of woman, born under the law, to redeem those who were under the law, so that we might receive adoption as sons" (Galatians 4:4-5).

In the devotion that follows, we'll try to unpack a little more of this mystery, but be clear in your mind that Jesus Christ, our Redeemer is One Person with two natures. He is 100% God and 100% man, as the Westminster Confession of Faith says, "without conversion, composition, or confusion."[12] That means His two natures are distinct and remain so even

---

12 *The Confession of Faith: Together with the Larger Catechism and Shorter Catechism* (Committee for Christian Education and Publications, PCA Bookstore: Atlanta, GA) 1990, p.29.

today, as He sits at His Father's right hand waiting to come again in glory.

Yes, our Redeemer is the "one mediator between God and men, the man Christ Jesus" (1 Timothy 2:5) because only one who is fully God and fully man can represent us in the covenant of grace and save us from our sins.

CHALLENGE QUESTIONS:

- Why is it necessary that Jesus is fully God (see Larger Catechism Question 38)?
- Why is it necessary that Jesus is fully man (see Larger Catechism Question 39)?

PRAYER:

Heavenly Father, thank you for sending a Redeemer, your own Son, to rescue us from our sins. Thank you that He is fully man and that He understands our sufferings and temptations. May we look to Him for help and hope as we wait for Him to come again. In Jesus' name we pray, Amen.

SHORTER CATECHISM
QUESTION 22

Q22 | HOW DID CHRIST, BEING THE SON OF GOD, BECOME MAN?

A.   Christ, the Son of God, became man, by taking to himself a true body, and a reasonable soul, being conceived by the power of the Holy Ghost, in the womb of the Virgin Mary, and born of her, yet without sin.

EXPLANATION:

I don't know what date you're reading this, but today is Christmas Day for you because we get to talk about the miracle of Christ's birth! I imagine you already know the story, how the angel Gabriel appeared to Mary in Nazareth and announced that she would give birth to a special child:

> "Do not be afraid, Mary, for you have found favor with God. And behold, you will conceive in your womb and bear a son, and you shall call His name Jesus. He will be

great and will be called the Son of the Most High. And the Lord God will give to him the throne of his father David, and... of his kingdom there shall be no end" (Luke 1:30-33).

What a wonderful promise! Mary will give birth to a King who will sit on David's throne, the long-awaited Messiah or Christ, the anointed One! And His name will be Jesus, which means Savior, "for He will save His people from their sins" (Matthew 1:21).

Of course, Mary didn't understand how she can give birth to the promised child because she was a virgin, not yet being married. But Gabriel reassured her:

"The Holy Spirit will come upon you, and the power of the Most High will overshadow you; therefore the child will be called holy – the Son of God....For nothing will be impossible with God" (Luke 1:35-37).

As we learned from Adam's fall, anyone born "by ordinary generation," or by a human father, is born into "an estate of sin and misery." If that were true of Jesus, He could not be our Savior. But because He is conceived by the Holy Spirit and born of the Virgin Mary, He is holy, "the lamb without blemish or spot" whose precious blood purifies us from sin (1 Peter 1:19).

And because Jesus was born of Mary, He has a true body. He doesn't just "seem" to be a man like a ghost, but the gospels tell us that He eats, drinks, sleeps, feels pain, and even dies. He also has a "reasonable soul," which means that He has a truly human mind and truly human emotions. The writer of Hebrews sums it up:

"Therefore he had to be made like his brothers in every respect, so that he might become a merciful and faithful high priest in the service of God, to make propitiation for the sins of the people. For because he himself has suffered when tempted, he is able to help those who are being tempted" (Hebrews 2:17-18).

Yes! Because "the Word became flesh and dwelt among us" (John 1:14), we can enjoy the miracle of Christmas all year long!

CHALLENGE QUESTIONS:

- Where in Scripture do we see proof that Jesus has a true body (John 20:24-28 or John 1:14)?

- Where do we find proof in Scripture that He has a true soul (Matthew 26:38)?

- Some say that the Virgin Birth of Jesus isn't possible and is only a myth. What happens to the Christian faith if Jesus had an earthly father?

PRAYER:

Gracious Father, thank You for the miracle of the Virgin Birth. Thank You for the sinless perfection of Jesus. Thank You that He's our Brother and Friend who knows what it's like to be human. We also thank You that He's Your Eternal Son, the Perfect God-Man, who is ever to be praised. In His name we pray, Amen.

SHORTER CATECHISM
QUESTION 23

Q23 | WHAT OFFICES DOTH CHRIST EXECUTE AS OUR REDEEMER?

A. Christ, as our Redeemer, executeth the offices of a prophet, of a priest, and of a king, both in his estate of humiliation and exaltation.

EXPLANATION:

You may have picked up in an earlier devotion that Christ is the New Testament word for Messiah. Both words mean "anointed one". Back in Old Testament days, there were three types of people who were anointed with oil to show that God had set them apart for special service: prophets, priests, and kings. Examples of prophets include Moses, Elijah, Isaiah, Jeremiah, Ezekiel, and Daniel. You probably know that Aaron and his sons were priests of Israel. The most famous kings of Israel were Saul, David, and Solomon. The Lord used each of these men in special ways to bless His people. And each one of them promised something to us about the Messiah to come. Prophets speak God's Word, priests offer sacrifices for sins, and kings rule over His people.

Yet, as we study the Old Testament, each one of these men falls short of saving God's people because of their sin and inability. Think of Moses, the greatest of the Old Testament prophets. He was a murderer (Exodus 2:14) and was reluctant to obey God because he was "slow of speech and of tongue" (Exodus 4:10). Yet, Moses promised the greater Prophet to come:

> "The LORD your God will raise up for you a prophet like me from among you, from your brothers—it is to him you shall listen...And I will put my words in his mouth, and he shall speak to them all that I command him" (Deuteronomy 18:15-18).

Think of the ways that High Priest Aaron fell short when crafting the golden calf and leading the people into idolatry (Exodus 32:2-6). One of the gravest sins in all of Scripture, it resulted in the deaths of 3,000 by the sword of their own brothers and many more through plague (Exodus 32:29, 35). Instead of taking away the sins of the people, Aaron "brought a great sin upon them" (Exodus 32:21). Even the atoning sacrifices of Aaron and his descendants had to be repeated each year, but his work as priest paints a picture of our Great High Priest, "who appeared once for all at the end of the ages to put away sin by the sacrifice of Himself" (Hebrews 9:26).

How about King David? We all know the horrible sins that he committed with Bathsheba, committing adultery, murdering her husband, and lying to cover all of it up. He failed to provide a good example, protect his people, and lead them with integrity. Yet, the LORD was faithful to keep His promise to David about the King to come:

> "I will raise up your offspring after you, who shall come from your body, and I will establish his kingdom. He shall build a house for my name, and I will establish the throne of his kingdom forever" (2 Samuel 7:12-13).

Yes. Jesus, our Redeemer, is the Christ, the Anointed One, our perfect Prophet, our perfect Priest, and our perfect King! And, as we'll see in the next three devotions, by executing these three offices, He saves us from our sins once and for all!

CHALLENGE QUESTIONS:

- Name some Old Testament prophets, priests, and kings NOT already mentioned above.
- How did they each fall short of perfection?

PRAYER:

Heavenly Father, thank You for Jesus, our Redeemer who died for our sins, who speaks truth, sacrificed Himself for our sins, and wisely rules over us as our King. May we listen to Him, pray in His name, and submit to Him today. In Jesus' name we pray, Amen.

SHORTER CATECHISM
QUESTION 24

Q24 | HOW DOTH CHRIST EXECUTE THE OFFICE OF A PROPHET?

A. Christ executeth the office of a prophet, in revealing to us, by His Word and Spirit, the will of God for our salvation.

EXPLANATION:

Do you remember way back in the tenth question we were told that God created Adam and Eve "in knowledge, righteousness, and holiness?" Well, because of Adam's sin, we all fell into ignorance, guilt, and sinfulness.[13] The good news is that Christ, our Redeemer, rescues us from all three!

Jesus rescues us from ignorance by being our Prophet. He reveals God's will to us for our salvation – not just how we come to faith – but also how we're supposed to live, and what

---

13 GI Williamson, *The Westminster Shorter Catechism for Study Classes* (Presbyterian and Reformed Publishing: Phillipsburg, NJ), 2003, p. 95.

we look forward to in heaven. As we heard last time, He is the Prophet greater than Moses. Not only does He proclaim like an Old Testament prophet, "Thus saith the Lord." He is the Lord! And His Spirit inspired the writing of Holy Scripture, including the Old Testament (1 Peter 1:10-11).

Jesus also speaks as prophet in New Testament times:

> "Long ago, at many times and in many ways, God spoke to our fathers by the prophets, but in these last days he has spoken to us by his Son" (Hebrews 1:1-2).

And Jesus stills speaks to us today when the Bible is read and preached. That's why Paul says, "faith comes from hearing, and hearing through the word of Christ" (Romans 10:17).

That means every time a preacher, teacher, or parent reads the Bible to us, Jesus speaks! The same thing is true when we read God's Word silently.

There is a problem, though. Because of our sin, on our own, we're like the people Isaiah describes. We hear, but don't understand. We see, but don't perceive. Our hearts are dull, our ears heavy, and our eyes blind (Isaiah 6:8-10). You see, "the natural man does not receive the things of the Spirit of God, for they are foolishness to him; nor can he know them, because they are spiritually discerned" (1 Corinthians 2:14).

But when Jesus, our Prophet sends His Holy Spirit, He makes our ears open to the gospel. He makes our eyes open to see Christ in the Scriptures. He makes our hearts alive so that we believe and want to obey! As Jesus promises:

> "When the Spirit of truth comes, he will guide you into all the truth" (John 16:13).

So let's remember to pray for the Holy Spirit's help when we come to the Scriptures, whether we're studying it on our own, attending a Bible Study, sharing it with our families, or hearing it preached in worship. Let's pray that the Spirit would open our ears so that we can hear Christ's crystal clear voice, and that He would deliver us from our ignorance and fill us with the wonderful knowledge of our salvation.

CHALLENGE QUESTIONS:

- How does Jesus speak to us today?
- Why do we need the Holy Spirit's help to understand the Bible?

PRAYER:

"May the Word of Christ dwell in us richly," (Colossians 3:16) O Lord. Holy Spirit, help us to hear Jesus speak to us. May He teach, reprove, correct, and train us in righteousness, that we might be complete, thoroughly equipped for every good work (2 Timothy 3:16, 17). In His name we pray, Amen.

SHORTER CATECHISM
QUESTION 25

Q25 | HOW DOTH CHRIST EXECUTE THE OFFICE OF A PRIEST?

A. Christ executeth the office of a priest, in His once offering up of himself a sacrifice to satisfy divine justice, and reconcile us to God; and in making continual intercession for us.

EXPLANATION:

One of my favorite Bible stories is that of Abraham climbing Mt. Moriah to sacrifice his son, Isaac. I know that may sound horrible; and it would have been, if the Angel of the LORD hadn't spoken to Abraham when he had raised his knife to sacrifice his son:

> "Abraham, Abraham!" And he said, "Here I am." He said, "Do not lay your hand on the boy or do anything to him... And Abraham lifted up his eyes and looked, and behold, behind him was a ram, caught in a thicket by his horns.

And Abraham went and took the ram and offered it up as a burnt offering instead of his son. So Abraham called the name of that place, "The LORD will provide"; as it is said to this day, "On the mount of the LORD it shall be provided" (Genesis 22:11-14).

Though Isaac deserves the just sentence of death because of his sins, our Heavenly Father provides a substitute, this ram caught in the thicket. In the same way, you and I deserve God's justice, His righteous judgment against our sins. But He has also provided a sacrifice, Jesus Christ, the Lamb of God. His death once and for all satisfied what God requires from us for our sins (Hebrews 9:12; 10:12).

You see, not only is Jesus the perfect sacrifice, He is also our Great High Priest! And just like the High Priest would do on the Day of Atonement, He atones for, or covers over, our sins by offering Himself! He does this in two ways that are illustrated by the two goats we read about in Leviticus 16. One we call the scapegoat:

"And Aaron shall lay both his hands on the head of the live goat, and confess over it all the iniquities of the people of Israel, and all their transgressions, all their sins. And he shall put them on the head of the goat and send it away into the wilderness.... (Leviticus 16:21-22).

Yes! Jesus is our Scapegoat! The theological word is "expiation", which means He removes our sins so that they are no longer held against us. He wipes our record clean:

"As far as the east is from the west, so far does he remove our transgressions from us" (Psalm 103:12).

The catechism also says that Jesus reconciles us to God. The theological word for this is "propitiation", which is illustrated by the other goat from the Day of Atonement. This one is killed and its blood Aaron sprinkles in the Holy of Holies. This blood temporarily satisfies God's anger as it points to Christ's blood. Aaron, is then allowed into God's holy presence to offer prayers on behalf of His people. What a beautiful picture of what Jesus does for us, "a propitiation by His blood (Romans 3:25)... making peace by the blood of His cross" (Colossians 1:20).

And not only does Jesus remove our sins and reconcile us to God through His death, the risen and ascended Christ also prays for us. He "always lives to make intercession for us" (Hebrews 7:25). What a "merciful and faithful high priest" (Hebrews 2:17)!

CHALLENGE QUESTIONS:

- How do the ram (Genesis 22) and the two goats (Leviticus 16) paint pictures of Jesus as our Great High Priest?

- How does it make you feel, knowing that Jesus is always praying for you?

PRAYER:

Heavenly Father, because Jesus has removed our sins and made peace with You, "let us with confidence draw near to the throne of grace, that we may receive mercy and find grace to help in time of need" (Hebrews 4:16). In His name we pray, Amen.

26

SHORTER CATECHISM
QUESTION 26

Q26 | HOW DOTH CHRIST EXECUTE THE OFFICE OF A KING?

A.   Christ executeth the office of a king, in subduing us to Himself, in ruling and defending us, and in restraining and conquering all His and our enemies.

EXPLANATION:

Do you feel encouraged and strengthened when you hear these words? You should! Our Redeemer, Jesus Christ is "King of kings and Lord of lords" (Revelation 19:16). He's the Almighty King who saved us in the past, who rules over us in the present, and who will finally deliver us in the future. Let's start with the past.

The catechism says He "subdued us to Himself." What does this mean? It means that Jesus captured our hearts. Remember, both by our nature and by our actions, we are sinful rebels, "foolish, disobedient, led astray" (Titus 3:3). But King Jesus "called us out of darkness into His marvelous light (1 Peter 2:9). That's right! He subdued us by His Word and Spirit, giving us new hearts so that we could believe in Him and repent, turning away from our sins! This is what He's done in the past for all of God's children.

In the present, Jesus rules over us. He does so through His Word. As Isaiah reports, "The LORD is our lawgiver, the LORD is our king" (Isaiah 33:22). And He ministers His Word through His church, through pastors and elders who are given "the keys of the kingdom of heaven" (Matthew 16:19). This means that they're responsible to keep doctrine pure, to keep watch over the flock, and to keep God's people on mission, making disciples of all nations (Matthew 28:16-20). Jesus also rules us through His Spirit,[14] as He convicts us of sin and conforms us into the image of our Redeemer.

Our King Jesus also defends us in the present. He keeps us safe! He is our "refuge and strength, a very *present* help in trouble" (Psalm 46:1). When we cry to Him for help, He hides us "under His wings" (Psalm 91:4). Nothing can touch us unless He allows it for our good and for His glory! Even though our enemies attack us, including Satan, King Jesus restrains them and conquers them so that we have nothing to fear, "for He will hide me in His shelter in the day of trouble...He will lift me high upon a rock" (Psalm 27:5).

What about the future? It's true that Satan sometimes wins against us. We fall to his temptations. We listen to his lies. We're discouraged and deflated when he accuses us. And those who

---

14 Thomas Vincent, *The Shorter Catechism Explained from Scripture* (The Banner of Truth Trust: 3 Murrayfield R., Edinburgh) 1980, p. 82.

follow him also persecute, oppress, and make fun of us. But, in the future, King Jesus will return. The conquering King will come in wrath, riding a white horse, eyes with flames of fire, head adorned with many crowns, his white robe dipped in the blood of His enemies, striking down the nations with the two-edged sword of His Word, and He will rule them forever with a rod of iron (Revelation 19:11-16). And He will throw Satan, along with His and our enemies, into the eternal lake of fire forever (Revelation 20:10. 14-15). Then, it will be our privilege to cast our crowns before our King Jesus (Revelation 4:16) who subdued us in the past, who rules and protects us now, and who will deliver us in the future.

CHALLENGE QUESTIONS:

- How does Jesus act as King in the past, present, and future?

- What areas in your life need to come under His rule?

- Why would it be encouraging to persecuted Christians that Jesus will conquer all their enemies?

PRAYER:

"Worthy is the Lamb who was slain, to receive power and wealth and wisdom and might and honor and glory and blessing" (Revelation 5:12). Thank You, King Jesus, for Your salvation – past, present, and future. In your name we pray, Amen.

SHORTER CATECHISM
QUESTION 27

Q27 | WHEREIN DID CHRIST'S HUMILIATION CONSIST?

A. Christ's humiliation consisted in His being born, and that in a low condition, made under the law, undergoing the miseries of this life, the wrath of God, and the cursed death of the cross; in being buried, and continuing under the power of death for a time.

EXPLANATION:

Over the last several days, we've studied the wonder of our Redeemer, our Messiah, the Anointed One who is Prophet, Priest, and King. When would we expect such an important Person, God's own Son, to enter the world? Born in a palace like a king, or in a temple like a priest, or in a university like a great teacher or prophet? No, the Bible paints a different picture, a picture of humility as God's Son takes on human flesh.

Christ's humiliation, or humbling, starts at His birth. Out of love for us and obedience to His Father, He doesn't "count equality with God a thing to be grasped" (Philippians 2:6). Instead, He willingly sets aside His heavenly glory for a time to be born "in the form of a servant, being born in the likeness of men." Now, it's important to remember that Jesus never loses His divinity. He remains fully God, even as He is conceived by the Holy Spirit and born of the Virgin Mary. Yet, during His life, He veils or covers His outward glory, though we see it shine through in His miracles, at the transfiguration, and most fully at His resurrection. But we see Him born not in a palace, temple, or university, but in a low condition, in a humble cattle stall to a poor young lady. Jesus is raised in what we would call a "working class" home. Truly, as Isaiah writes:

> "He grew up before Him like a young plant, and like a root of dry ground; He had no form or majesty that we should look at Him, and no beauty that we should desire Him" (Isaiah 53:2).

The catechism also tells us that Jesus is "made under the law," even though He is the One who actually made the law! We know that He obeyed the law perfectly, though He was "tempted as we are, yet without sin" (Hebrews 4:15).

Another way Jesus shows us His humility is in "undergoing the miseries of this life." Since Jesus is fully human, He cried when He was a baby in Bethlehem, bled when He skinned His knee in Nazareth, and experienced fatigue, hunger, thirst, and pain as He walked through Judea during His ministry. Scripture calls Him a "man of sorrows, acquainted with grief" (Isaiah 53:3). And Jesus is most miserable in body and soul through His sufferings leading up to His death: praying in the Garden of Gethsemane, being betrayed by Judas, being tried and brutally beaten by the Jews and Romans, and as He carries the cross to Golgotha, and is stripped of His clothes.

Yes, Paul tells us that "He humbled Himself by being obedient to the point of death, even death on a cross" (Philippians 2:8). Think of it! The One who is Life (John 11:25; 14:6) dies in our place! And not only does He die, but He was wrapped and buried in a tomb, the very One who made Adam out of the dust of the earth! And He stays in the Garden Tomb for three days.

"What wondrous love is this?" That God's Son, our glorious Redeemer, would humble Himself "to seek and save the lost" (Luke 19:10).

CHALLENGE QUESTIONS:

- Name some of the ways that Jesus humbles Himself. How does it help you to know that Jesus understands what it's like to feel pain?
- To be humiliated?
- To be rejected?
- To be tempted (Hebrews 4:15)?

PRAYER:

Thank You, Jesus, for humbling Yourself to be born, to be the New Adam who obeyed perfectly even under temptation, who died in our place, and who was buried. May we have confidence to pray for Your help when life is hard here on earth because we know You have walked in our shoes. In your name we pray, Amen.

SHORTER CATECHISM
QUESTION 28

Q28 | WHEREIN CONSISTETH CHRIST'S EXALTATION?

A. Christ's exaltation consisteth in His rising again from the dead on the third day, in ascending up into heaven, in sitting at the right hand of God the Father, and in coming to judge the world at the last day.

EXPLANATION:

Exaltation may be an unfamiliar word to you. We don't use it all that often in everyday language. But it means to be lifted up. Your parents or grandparents probably exalt you on your birthday by seating you in a special place, presenting you with a beautifully decorated cake, and singing "Happy Birthday to you!" Or maybe you've been recognized as a good student, athlete, musician, or leader with an award. These are times when we are exalted or "lifted up" in the eyes of people. Something like this happens when God the Father exalts our

Lord Jesus Christ. Following His humiliation, which ended in His "obedience, even to the point of death, even death on a cross," Paul tells us:

> "God has highly exalted Him and bestowed on Him the name that is above every name" (Philippians 2:8-9).

We might say that Christ's exaltation or lifting up takes place in several stages, each stage being more glorious than the one before! It begins on the third day after His death: "He was buried, (and) he was raised on the third day in accordance with the Scriptures"(1 Corinthians 15:4).

Jesus proves that He is the Son of God (Romans 1:4) and that our sins are paid for by His bodily resurrection from the dead (Romans 4:25). And we must believe that He rose again in order to be saved. If not, Paul says, "your faith is futile, and you are still in your sins" (1 Corinthians 15:17). But we know that Jesus did rise again as He "appeared to Cephas (Peter), then to the twelve" and to over five hundred Christians at one time (1 Corinthians 15:4-5). He even let the Apostles touch His risen body and ate with them, proving that they weren't merely seeing a spirit or a ghost (Luke 24:39-43).

The next stage of His exaltation, His ascension, happened forty days after He rose again. Jesus is lifted up in front of His Apostles in the town of Bethany, near Jerusalem: "And when he had said these things, as they were looking on, he was lifted up, and a cloud took him out of their sight" (Acts 1:9).

We know, too, that Jesus sits at a high and exalted place – at the "right hand of God" (Heb. 1:3; 10:12; 12:2). This means that He is ruling over and defending us as our Mighty King (see Q 26) and praying for us as our Great High Priest (see Q 25).

But His greatest exaltation is yet to come! He will appear once again and every person who has ever walked the earth will bow down before the exalted Christ: "...at the name of Jesus every knee should bow, in heaven and on earth and under the earth, and every tongue confess that Jesus Christ is Lord, to the glory of God the Father" (Philippians 2:10-11).

The question is: Will you bow in terror, knowing that He will cast you into the eternal lake of fire? Or will you bow in worship, rejoicing in the exalted Christ who will take you to His Father's house?

CHALLENGE QUESTIONS:

- What does Christ's resurrection prove?
- How does He help us now that He's ascended to the Father?
- How can we be ready for His second coming?

PRAYER:

"Oh magnify the LORD with me, and let us exalt His name together (Psalm 34:3). We lift up your name, Christ Jesus, for You are the risen, ascended, ruling and reigning King. We look forward to the day when you come again. May we be found ready when you return. In your exalted name we pray, Amen.

SHORTER CATECHISM
QUESTIONS 29 & 30

Q29 | **HOW ARE WE MADE PARTAKERS OF THE REDEMPTION PURCHASED BY CHRIST?**

A.   We are made partakers of the redemption purchased by Christ by the effectual application of it to us by His Holy Spirit.

EXPLANATION:

So far, in our studies, we've learned about the glorious character of our Triune God: Father, Son, and Holy Spirit. We've looked at God's works of creation and providence. We've seen man's fall into sin and the horrible consequences that followed. Most recently, we've discussed Jesus Christ our Redeemer, our perfect Prophet, Priest, and King in His states of humiliation and exaltation. Paul describes the very center of His saving work in Ephesians 1:7:

"In him we have redemption through his blood, the forgiveness of our trespasses, according to the riches of his grace" (Ephesians 1:7).

For the next several questions, the catechism shifts its focus to how God connects us to the saving work of Jesus. He does so by His gracious and powerful Holy Spirit. As question 30 explains:

Q30 | HOW DOTH THE SPIRIT APPLY TO US THE REDEMPTION PURCHASED BY CHRIST?

A. **The Spirit applieth to us the redemption purchased by Christ by working faith in us, and thereby uniting us to Christ in our effectual calling.**

EXPLANATION:

What a reminder that our union with Christ, our inseparable relationship with Him (Ephesians 1:3-14), is not something that we earn. Even our faith that connects us to Him is a gift of God (Ephesians 2:8-9). We'll get into the "nuts and bolts" of how all of this happens in the days ahead, but let's take this opportunity to praise the Holy Spirit for His work in uniting us to Christ! Consider Paul's words:

"But when the goodness and loving kindness of God our Savior appeared, he saved us, not because of works done by us in righteousness, but according to his own mercy, by the washing of regeneration and renewal of the Holy Spirit, whom he poured out on us richly through Jesus Christ our Savior, so that being justified by his grace we might become heirs according to the hope of eternal life" (Titus 3:4-7).

Let us never forget that our salvation in Christ is all of grace!

CHALLENGE QUESTIONS:

- Why is Titus 3:4-7 a good summary of the gospel?
- Who applies Christ's redemption to us?
- How would you define union with Christ (John 15:1-11)?
- Can our union with Christ ever be broken (John 10:27-29; Rom. 8:37-39)?

PRAYER:

May *"the God of all grace, who has called us to his eternal glory in Christ, restore, confirm, strengthen, and establish us" (1 Pet. 5:10) as we seek His Holy Spirit to live for His glory. In Jesus' name we pray, Amen.*

31

SHORTER CATECHISM
QUESTION 31

Q.31 | WHAT IS EFFECTUAL CALLING?

A.   Effectual calling is the work of God's Spirit,
whereby, convincing us of our sin and misery,
enlightening our minds in the knowledge of
Christ, and renewing our wills, He doth persuade
and enable us to embrace Jesus Christ freely
offered to us in the gospel.

EXPLANATION:

Has your mother ever called you for supper, but you didn't
hear her because you were listening to music, or watching
a video, or playing a game with earbuds in? No matter how
loudly she yelled, you didn't respond! Maybe everyone
else heard her, but you couldn't because your ears were
all stopped up. That's what it's like for those who cannot
hear the gospel because of their sinful natures. And it's
not just their ears. It's their eyes and their hearts as well

(Isaiah 6:8-10). But everything changes when the Holy Spirit effectually, or effectively, calls a sinner to salvation!

How does the Spirit call us? He begins by convincing us of our sin and misery. As we've said before, we must be convinced of our diagnosis, our sinful condition, before we're ready to receive the medicine Christ offers in His gospel. We see evidence of this in Peter's sermon at Pentecost. After preaching to the very people who rejected and crucified Jesus, we read:

> "Now when they heard this they were cut to the heart and said.... 'Brothers, what shall we do? And Peter said to them, 'Repent and be baptized every one of you in the name of Jesus Christ for the forgiveness of your sins..."(Acts 2:37-38).

The Spirit also "enlightens our minds in the knowledge of Christ." Not only does He convince us of the bad news, He graciously opens our hearts to believe the good news! I love the story of Lydia, the first person to believe the gospel in Europe. While she's attending a prayer meeting by the riverside in Philippi, "The Lord opened her heart to pay attention to what was said by Paul" (Acts 16:14) as he preached the good news about Jesus. Yes. It is the Spirit who "opens our eyes, turns us from darkness to light, and from the power of Satan to God" (Acts 26:18).

Another thing the Spirit does is renew our wills. Sometimes we say that He gives us new hearts. This is called "regeneration" or "rebirth". Jesus speaks about this to Nicodemus: "Truly, truly, I say to you, unless one is born of water and the Spirit, he cannot enter the kingdom of God...You must be born again. The wind blows where it wishes, and you hear its sound, but you do not know where it comes from or where it goes. So it is with everyone who is born of the Spirit" (John 3:5-8).

And once the Spirit renews our wills (but not until then!), we're free to embrace, to trust in Jesus as He's "freely offered to us in the gospel." As Jesus explains in John 6:

> "All that the Father gives me will come to me, and whoever comes to me I will never cast out...No one can come to me unless the Father who sent me draws him" (John 6:37, 44).

How good is the Holy Spirit to take those who were dead in sin and transgression and make them alive in Christ, complete with opened eyes that see, unstopped ears that hear the good news, and new hearts that trust in Christ alone for salvation!

CHALLENGE QUESTIONS:

- Can you think of a time when a parent called you, but you didn't hear them?
- Why do we need new hearts before we can believe?

PRAYER:

Gracious Father, thank you for sending the Holy Spirit who causes us "to be born again to a living hope" (1 Peter 1:3). May we "walk in newness of life" (Romans 6:4) as we serve Jesus today. In His name we pray, Amen.

SHORTER CATECHISM
QUESTIONS 32 & 33

Q.32 | WHAT BENEFITS DO THEY THAT ARE EFFECTUALLY CALLED PARTAKE OF IN THIS LIFE?

A. They that are effectually called do in this life partake of justification, adoption, and sanctification, and the several benefits which in this life do either accompany or flow from them.

EXPLANATION:

Did you know that the moment the Spirit effectually calls us our new life in Christ begins? Once we respond to Him in faith and repentance of our sins, His unbreakable union with us is set forever. And there is so much that God gives us as a result, things that He's planned to give His children from before the foundation of the world. He delights to give us "every spiritual blessing in the heavenly places" (Ephesians 1:3). These are the kinds of blessings we read about in the answer to question 32. We'll talk about the first one today.

Q33 | WHAT IS JUSTIFICATION?

A.   Justification is an act of God's free grace, wherein He pardoneth all our sins, and accepteth us as righteous in His sight, only for the righteousness of Christ imputed to us, and received by faith alone.

EXPLANATION:

Justification is a big word. You may have heard that justification means "just as if I had never sinned." And that's right! Probably the best way to understand justification is to think of a court room. Justification is a legal decision. Imagine a guilty person standing before a righteous judge.[15] We're like that guilty person because all of us have sinned and fall short of God's glory (Romans 3:23). We deserve the wages of sin, which is eternal death in hell (Romans 6:23). But the judge, our holy God, declares once and for all from the bench, "Not Guilty!" This includes sins we've committed in the past, the ones we're committing in the present, and even the ones we'll commit in the future.

How can this be? God the Father imputes or transfers our guilty record to Jesus, His Son: "The LORD has laid on him the iniquity of us all" (Isaiah 53:6). He then transfers His perfect record of righteousness to us: "by the one man's obedience the many will be made righteous" (Romans 5:19). Paul summarizes this amazing transaction in 2 Corinthians:

---

15 GI Williamson, *The Westminster Shorter Catechism for Study Classes* (Presbyterian and Reformed Publishing: Phillipsburg, NJ), 2003, p. 148.

"For our sake he made him to be sin who knew no sin, so that in him we might become the righteousness of God" (2 Corinthians 5:21).

Now keep in mind, justification is an act of God's free grace. It's a gift. We can do nothing to earn it, not even by trying hard to be "a good person," or going to church, or putting lots of money in the offering plate. Instead, we receive it by faith in Jesus Christ alone. As we read in Galatians:

"Yet we know that a person is not justified by works of the law but through faith in Jesus Christ...because by works of the law no one will be justified" (Galatians 2:16).

Has God pardoned your sins and accepted you as righteous? He will if you believe in Christ Jesus!

CHALLENGE QUESTIONS:

- How can sinners be declared righteous?
- What are some ways people try to earn forgiveness on their own?
- Why does knowing that God has justified us in Christ comfort us when we sin?

PRAYER:

"Who shall bring any charge against God's elect? It is God who justifies" (Romans 8:33). Gracious Father, thank You for sending Jesus to remove the guilt of our sins once and for all. In His name we pray, Amen.

SHORTER CATECHISM
QUESTION 34

Q34 | WHAT IS ADOPTION?

A. Adoption is an act of God's free grace, whereby we are received into the number, and have a right to all the privileges of the sons of God.

EXPLANATION:

Were you or someone in your family adopted? Maybe you have a friend or know someone at school or church who is adopted. Adoption is special because parents, out of their great love, specially choose children who don't have a home and invite them into their families. The same is true for our loving Heavenly Father who has adopted us into His royal family!

Think of what God has done. Because of Adam's sin, "we were by nature children of wrath..." (Ephesians 2:3). We were spiritual orphans, enslaved by Satan. But "in love, He predestined us for adoption as sons through Jesus Christ"

(Ephesians 1:4-5). Now, after we've believed in Christ and repented of our sins, we've been received into the number of God's family. We belong to "the assembly of the firstborn who are enrolled in heaven" (Hebrews 12:23). Did you hear that? All Christians – male and female – are considered firstborn sons. And just like the Old Testament days, we receive a double portion of the Father's riches. As Paul writes, we are "children of God, and if children, then heirs – heirs of God and fellow heirs with Christ" (Romans 8:16-17).

So what are some of the privileges that we enjoy as God's children?

We have the privilege of a new name, a new identity. We are His new creations in Christ (2 Corinthians 5:17). Jesus tells us: "I will write on him the name of my God, and the name of the city of my God, the new Jerusalem....and my own new name" (Revelation 3:12). We no longer belong to the world; we belong to Jesus and we're citizens of heaven!

We have the privilege of the Holy Spirit, who assures us of our salvation when we doubt God's love. As Paul writes: "... you have received the Spirit of adoption as sons, by whom we cry, 'Abba! Father!' The Spirit Himself bears witness with our spirit that we are children of God" (Romans 8:15, 16). "Abba" means something like Papa or Daddy – so warm is God's love toward us!

We have the privilege of prayer. Our Heavenly Father wants to hear what's on our hearts as we pray in Jesus' name. And even when we're weak and don't know how or what to pray, "the Spirit Himself intercedes for us with groanings too deep for words....because the Spirit intercedes for the saints according to the will of God" (Romans 8:26-27)

We have the privilege of discipline. That may sound funny, but one of the ways we know that God is our Father is that He disciplines us like a good earthly father. He doesn't do this to be harsh or mean, but to correct us "for our good, that we may share in His holiness" (Hebrews 12:10).

We have the privilege of fellowship. When we receive the Lord's Supper, all of God's redeemed children are invited to eat and drink with Him for a family meal. Christ, our older brother, is our host. All of this is just a taste of what it will be like when we are welcomed into our Father's house, where Jesus is preparing a place for us now (John 14:1-2).

Is there any higher privilege than to be adopted into the family of God?

CHALLENGE QUESTIONS:

- Do you know anyone who has been adopted?
- Name some of the privileges we enjoy as God's children.

PRAYER:

"Behold what manner of love the Father has bestowed upon us, that we should be called children of God" (1 John 3:1). Heavenly Father, thank you for loving us in Christ and for all of the unending blessings you give to your children every day. In Jesus' name we pray, Amen.

35

SHORTER CATECHISM
QUESTION 35

Q35 | WHAT IS SANCTIFICATION?

A. Sanctification is the work of God's free grace, whereby we are renewed in the whole man after the image of God, and are enabled more and more to die unto sin, and live unto righteousness.

EXPLANATION:

In our last devotion, we talked about the privileges of adoption. One of the wonderful things that happens to us when our Heavenly Father adopts us is that we begin to bear the family resemblance. We begin to look like our Lord Jesus Christ. The more we walk with Him, the more we think like Him, talk like Him, and act like Him. This is what we call "sanctification". You may notice that this word is a bit like the word sanctuary, a holy place where we worship. Well, that's what it means. It's God's gracious work in us to make us holy, like He is holy (1 Peter 1:16).

Do you remember when we were talking about Adam's fall? How every single part of him (along with all people after him) was contaminated by sin? God's work of sanctification restores what was ruined in the fall and "conforms us into the image of His Son" (Romans 8:29). And this is a lifelong process. It's an ongoing work. It's not like justification and adoption which are one-time acts. Sanctification is the process of becoming holy. It's God's work of free grace within us: "For this is the will of God, your sanctification" (1 Thessalonians 4:3).

One thing we must remember about sanctification: God invites us to join Him in this work of becoming like Jesus. As Paul writes, "Therefore, my beloved, as you have always obeyed...work out your own salvation with fear and trembling" (Philippians 2:12). The Bible tells us that we're to die to sin because it no longer has control over us (Romans 6:8-10). Paul tells us to "put to death therefore what is earthly in you: sexual immorality, impurity, passion, evil desire, and covetousness, which is idolatry" (Colossians 3:5). This means that we starve our sins. We run away from them. We cut them out of our thoughts, words, and actions.

Not only are we to "die more and more unto sin," we're to "live unto righteousness." We're to "put on...as God's chosen ones, holy and beloved, compassionate hearts, kindness, humility, meekness, and patience...and above all these, put on love" (Colossians 3:12-14). We're to "put on the new self, which is being renewed in knowledge after the image of our Creator" (Colossians 3:10).

Of course, we can't die to sin and live to righteousness on our own. Remember that it is "God who works in [us] both to will and to work for His good pleasure" (Philippians 2:13). And He especially works when we behold His glory – in worship, in His Word, and in prayer. And though we still do battle with remaining sin, when we meet with the Lord Jesus, we "are being transformed into [His] image from one degree of glory to another. For this comes from the Lord who is the Spirit" (2 Corinthians 3:18).

This is the work of sanctification that our God has begun in each one of us and He will be faithful to complete it (Philippians 1:6) until we're the spitting image of our Savior!

CHALLENGE QUESTIONS:

- What does sanctification mean?

- How does the story of Joseph and Potiphar's wife show us what it looks like to run away from sin (Genesis 39:1-18)?

- How does the story of David and Bathsheba show the opposite (2 Samuel 11:1-5)?

PRAYER:

Holy Father, make us holy as you are holy. Help us to turn away from our sins. Renew our minds and help us to think about what is "true, honorable, just, pure, lovely, commendable, excellent, and praiseworthy" (Philippians 4:8). May our words and our actions also reflect the glory of your Son. In His name we pray, Amen.

SHORTER CATECHISM
QUESTION 36

Q36 | **WHAT ARE THE BENEFITS WHICH IN THIS LIFE DO ACCOMPANY OR FLOW FROM JUSTIFICATION, ADOPTION, AND SANCTIFICATION?**

A. The benefits which in this life do accompany or flow from justification, adoption, and sanctification, are, assurance of God's love, peace of conscience, joy in the Holy Ghost, increase of grace, and perseverance therein to the end.

EXPLANATION:

Have you ever gone to one of those all-you-can eat buffets? Or have you seen on a restaurant's menu: bottomless fries, free refills, or never-ending pasta bowl? Those are great places to go if you're hungry because there is no limit to the amount of food you can eat. Well, there are a couple of limits - the amount of food stored up at the restaurant, and more importantly, the capacity of your stomach! We might say that God's benefits and blessings are like this for His justified, adopted, and sanctified children, except there truly are no limits! For God has "blessed us in Christ with every spiritual blessing in the heavenly places" (Ephesians 1:3)?

The answer to question 36 names several of these blessings. Things like love, peace, joy, and assurance of what happens when we die. Have you ever considered that these are the very things our culture longs for and works so hard to achieve? Sadly, those who don't know Christ can never really enjoy these blessings in their fullness. They may catch a glimpse of them, but it never lasts.

On the other hand, all of God's children enjoy all of His benefits. Even if we sometimes forget that to experience them, all we have to do is ask. Paul speaks about them in Romans:

"Therefore, since we have been justified by faith, we have peace with God through our Lord Jesus Christ. Through him we have also obtained access by faith into this grace in which we stand, and we rejoice in hope of the glory of God. Not only that, but we rejoice in our sufferings, knowing that suffering produces endurance, and endurance produces character, and character produces hope, and hope does not put us to shame, because God's love has been poured into our hearts through the Holy Spirit who has been given to us" (Romans 5:1-5).

And the best news is that our enjoyment of these benefits increases throughout our lives and can never be taken away from us. They and we will persevere to the end!

CHALLENGE QUESTIONS:

- Read through the answer to Question 36 again. Which of these benefits are you enjoying the most right now?

- Which ones do you wish you were enjoying more?

- What should we do when we're lacking in assurance, peace and joy?

PRAYER:

Heavenly Father, may we bless your holy name. May we not forget all of your benefits, for you "forgive all our iniquity, heal all our diseases. You've redeemed our lives from the pit, and you crown our lives with steadfast love and mercy, satisfying us with good so that our youth is renewed like the eagle's" (Psalm 103:3-5). We pray in Jesus' name, Amen.

SHORTER CATECHISM
QUESTION 37

Q37 | WHAT BENEFITS DO BELIEVERS RECEIVE FROM CHRIST AT DEATH?

A. The souls of believers are at their death made perfect in holiness, and do immediately pass into glory; and their bodies, still united to Christ, do rest in their graves till the resurrection.

EXPLANATION:

"What happens when I die?" Have you ever asked that question? You're surely not alone as people – from the youngest child to the oldest sage – have pondered this question since time began. Obviously, for those who don't know Jesus as Savior, this is a troubling and even terrifying question. But for the believer, even though we know that death is an enemy that entered the world through Adam's sin, there is great comfort because Jesus takes care of our souls and our bodies when we die.

In terms of our souls, we know Paul's words: "To be absent from the body is to be present with the Lord" (2 Corinthians 5:8). At our death, immediately after we've taken our final breath, we'll be in the glorious presence of Jesus in His Father's house (John 14:2). We'll be there with all the saints who've died since righteous Abel, along with the angels who serve and sing around God's throne. And we'll all be changed! When we die, our souls or "spirits" are "made perfect" (Hebrews 12:23). God's work of sanctification, of making us holy, will be complete as we'll be fully "conformed to the image of Christ."[16] That means there will no longer be anything sinful in us!

How about our bodies? Don't they just waste away in the grave? No! Not at all! The Bible tells us that believers, at our death, "sleep in Jesus" (1 Thessalonians 4:14), meaning that He hasn't forgotten our bodies.[17] Our bodies belong to Him and He has a wonderful plan for them when He comes again at the Last Day. This is what we hope and long for – the final and fullest stage of our salvation!

> "...for an hour is coming when all who are in the tombs will hear his voice and come out, those who have done good to the resurrection of life, and those who have done evil to the resurrection of judgment" (John 5:28-29).

Yes, Jesus Himself "will descend from heaven with a cry of command, with the voice of an archangel, and with the sound of the trumpet of God. And the dead in Christ will rise first" (1 Thessalonians 4:16).

---

16 Thomas Vincent, *The Shorter Catechism Explained from Scripture* (The Banner of Truth Trust: 3 Murrayfield R., Edinburgh) 1980, p. 102.

17 Gl Williamson, *The Westminster Shorter Catechism for Study Classes* (Presbyterian and Reformed Publishing: Phillipsburg, NJ), 2003, p. 173

Since Jesus cares this much for our bodies in life and in death, this means that we should care for them while we live. We should treat them as temples of the Holy Spirit (1 Corinthians 6:19). We should not present our bodies "to sin as instruments for unrighteousness, but (instead) present ourselves to God as those who have been brought from death to life, and our members to God as instruments for righteousness" (Romans 6:13). And as Nicodemus and Joseph of Arimathea honored Jesus' body at His death and burial (John 19:38-42), so we should treat the bodies of His people with the same respect when they die. For we belong to Jesus – body and soul – in life and in death!

CHALLENGE QUESTIONS:

- What are some common things you've heard non-Christians say about what happens at death?
- What does the Bible say happens to our souls when we die?
- What about our bodies?

PRAYER:

Thank you, Heavenly Father, that you save us body and soul. Though death is our enemy, we thank you that you've given us new life through your Spirit and the hope of heavenly glory to come for our souls and our bodies. In Jesus' name, Amen.

SHORTER CATECHISM
QUESTION 38

Q 38 | WHAT BENEFITS DO BELIEVERS RECEIVE FROM CHRIST AT THE RESURRECTION?

A.   At the resurrection, believers, being raised up in glory, shall be openly acknowledged and acquitted in the day of judgment, and made perfectly blessed in the full enjoying of God to all eternity.

EXPLANATION:

Many people (even some faithful Christians!) think that they receive their full heavenly inheritance when they die. They think that enjoying a glorified soul in God's presence is as good as it gets. But Jesus came to give us so much more! The Risen Christ is "the firstfuits of those who have fallen asleep [died in Christ]" (1 Corinthians 15:20). And just as Jesus's body rose in glory on the third day, so too will our bodies rise in glory when He comes again at the Last Day:

"So is it with the resurrection of the dead. What is sown is perishable; what is raised is imperishable. It is sown in dishonor; it is raised in glory. It is sown in weakness; it is raised in power. It is sown a natural body; it is raised a spiritual body. If there is a natural body, there is also a spiritual body" (1 Corinthians 15:42-44).

Do you hear this good news? Though Adam's sin left our bodies perishable (able to die), dishonorable, and weak, when the last trumpet sounds, our bodies will be changed in an instant, "in the twinkling of an eye" (1 Corinthians 15:52)! The physical bodies that we're now living in will be transformed so that they're imperishable, glorious, and powerful. Gone will be aches and pains. Gone will be weakness of eyes, ears, and mind. Gone will be disease and death – forever! We'll be made like the risen, glorified Jesus:

"Beloved, we are God's children now, and what we will be has not yet appeared; but we know that when he appears we shall be like him, because we shall see him as he is (1 John 3:2).

You may know that both believers and unbelievers will rise when Jesus comes again. As our Lord prophesies:

"....an hour is coming when all who are in the tombs will hear his voice and come out, those who have done good to the resurrection of life, and those who have done evil to the resurrection of judgment" (John 5:28-29).

It is true: "we must all appear before the judgment seat of Christ" (2 Corinthians 5:10). Jesus will judge us on our works, whether good or bad. Those deeds we've done that aren't built on Christ's foundation will be burned up in judgment.

We'll also be rewarded for those things we've done that honor Him (1 Corinthians 3:11-15) because they bring glory to Him and prove that we are truly His children.

Remember, the catechism tells us that we "shall be openly acknowledged and acquitted in the day of judgment." You see, true believers in Christ have no fear of missing out on our heavenly inheritance as Jesus will say to us:

> "Well done, good and faithful servant...enter into the joy of your master...Come, you who are blessed by my Father, inherit the kingdom prepared for you from the foundation of the world (Matthew 25:23, 34).

And best of all, we'll get to enjoy "face-to-face" fellowship with the Triune God and explore the joyful pleasures of His kingdom (Psalm 16:11) in the fullness of who God created us to be – body and soul forever!

CHALLENGE QUESTIONS:

- How will Christ's judgment be similar for believers and unbelievers?

- How will it be different?

- Read Revelation 21:3-4. Which of these blessings are you most looking forward to?

PRAYER:

Heavenly Father, though we only see your glory "in a mirror dimly," give us the hope that we will one day see you face to face (1 Corinthians 13:12). This we ask in Jesus' name, Amen.

SHORTER CATECHISM
QUESTIONS 39-42

Q39 | WHAT IS THE DUTY WHICH GOD REQUIRETH OF MAN?

A. The duty which God requireth of man is obedience to His revealed will.

EXPLANATION:

Today, we start a new section of the catechism. The first 38 questions were about what we're to believe concerning God. From Question 39 to the end, we'll discover "what duty God requires of man" (See Question 3). We're going to see that God has revealed His will to us. He has shown us how we're supposed to live for His glory (Micah 6:8). This is true for everyone who has ever lived, starting with Adam. As Question 40 asks:

Q40 | WHAT DID GOD AT FIRST REVEAL TO MAN FOR THE RULE OF HIS OBEDIENCE?

A.   The rule which God at first revealed to man for his obedience, was the moral law.

EXPLANATION:

We know that God spoke to Adam in the Garden of Eden, revealing to him what he required for eternal life – perfect obedience to His law. And after the fall, He also spoke to people like Cain, Noah, Abraham, Isaac, and Jacob. He then told Moses and the Prophets to write down His laws so that His people could read them, hear them taught, believe them, and obey them. What about those who've never heard God speak or read His Word? How do they know what God requires of them? Paul tells us that "the work of the law is written on their hearts" (Romans 2:15), their consciences "bearing witness" that they know right from wrong. This is God's moral law.

Q41 | WHERE IS THE MORAL LAW SUMMARILY COMPREHENDED?

A.   The moral law is summarily comprehended (or summarized) in the ten commandments.

EXPLANATION:

You remember how God spoke His holy law to Moses and the people from Mt. Sinai, accompanied by "thunder and the flashes of lightning and the sound of the trumpet and the mountain smoking" (Exodus 20:18). Now some laws we find in the Old Testament we are no longer required to obey, like those involving animal sacrifices. However, God's moral law summarized in the ten commandments is still our guide for holy living. They are so important that God wrote them with His own finger on tablets of stone! We will look at all ten very carefully over the next several devotions. But Question 42 gives us a great overview of what's in them.

Q42 | WHAT IS THE SUM OF THE TEN COMMANDMENTS?

A. The sum of the ten commandments is, "To love the LORD our God with all our heart, with all our soul, and with all our strength, and with all our mind; and our neighbor as ourselves."

EXPLANATION:

Jesus quoted these very words from the Old Testament (Deuteronomy 6:5; Leviticus 19:18) to the lawyer who asked Him, "Teacher, which is the greatest commandment in the law" (Matthew 22:36)? He ended his response by saying, "On these two commandments depend all the Law and the Prophets."

Think of the ten commandments divided between two stone tablets. On top of the first is written "Love God." Underneath, we can write the first four commandments because they teach us how to love and worship God. On the top of the second tablet is written "Love your Neighbor," and underneath we can write the last six commandments which teach us how to love one another. In other words, we can sum up what God requires of us by saying "Love God and love your neighbor."

CHALLENGE QUESTIONS:

- How does God reveal Himself even to those who've never read the Bible (Romans 2:14-15)?
- Can you remember and recite the ten commandments?
- How can we summarize them?

PRAYER:

"Open our eyes, Lord, that we may behold wondrous things out of your law" (Psalm 119:18). Help us to love you and our neighbor. In Jesus' name, we pray, Amen.

SHORTER CATECHISM
QUESTIONS 43 & 44

Q43 | WHAT IS THE PREFACE TO THE TEN COMMANDMENTS?

A. The preface to the ten commandments is in these words, 'I am the Lord thy God, which have brought thee out of the land of Egypt, out of the house of bondage.'"

EXPLANATION:

When you open a book, you'll usually find a preface after the table of contents. A preface is like an introduction from the author. In the preface to the ten commandments, God introduces Himself and gives us three reasons why we should obey Him.

Q44 | WHAT DOTH THE PREFACE TO THE TEN COMMANDMENTS TEACH US?

A. The preface to the ten commandments teacheth us, that because God is the Lord, and our God and Redeemer, therefore we are bound to keep all His commandments.

EXPLANATION:

The first reason we should read and obey the ten commandments is because God is the Lord. He is King and we are subjects (Psalm 96:7-9). He is Creator and we are creatures (Psalm 100:3). Therefore, we owe Him our obedience. As Solomon reminds us, "Fear God and keep his commandments, for this is the whole duty of man" (Ecclesiastes 12:13). We obey God because it's our duty.

And not only is He the Lord, He is OUR God! That's the second reason we should obey Him. You see, He's the one who has loved us and chosen us to be His children from before the foundation of the world (Ephesians 1:4-5). He's the one who feeds, clothes, and takes care of every one of our needs (Matthew 6:25-34). And He gives us His commandments to live by because, as our loving Father, He knows what's best for us. As He tells us, "Oh that they had such a heart....to fear me and to keep all my commandments, that it might go well with them and with their descendants forever" (Deuteronomy 5:29). The opposite is true, too – when we disobey Him, it won't go well with us. We obey God because it's for our good.

But there's a third and final reason to obey His commandments and it's the most wonderful. He is our Redeemer. This is what we see pictured in Israel's miraculous deliverance from Egypt. As He tells the Israelites: "You yourselves have seen what I did to the Egyptians, and how I bore you on eagles' wings and brought you to myself" (Exodus 19:4). Our mighty God redeemed Israel "out of the land of Egypt, out of the house of bondage" through the blood of the Passover Lamb, through His powerful parting of the Red Sea, and through His defeat of Pharaoh's army. We, as Christians know, too, that we've been redeemed through the true Passover Lamb, our Lord Jesus Christ, who shed His precious blood. We obey Him out of love and gratitude for our redemption.

And now that we've been delivered from our sins, our Lord doesn't want us to slide back into slavery by going back to our old ways. Instead, He wants us to live in freedom!

> "But thanks be to God, that you who were once slaves of sin have become obedient from the heart to the standard of teaching to which you were committed, and, having been set free from sin, have become slaves of righteousness" (Romas 6:17-18).

That's why the Lord our God, our Redeemer, gave us these commandments – because He loves us. And if we love Him, we will keep His commandments (John 14:15).

CHALLENGE QUESTIONS:

- Do you typically stop to read the preface of books?

- Why or why not?

- Read the preface to the ten commandments again. What reasons does God give for us to obey Him?

PRAYER:

"Oh how we love your law, we meditate on it all the day" (Psalm 119:97). Give us hearts to love and obey you, glorious Lord, gracious God, loving Redeemer. This we pray in Jesus' name, Amen.

SHORTER CATECHISM
QUESTIONS 45-47

Q45 | WHICH IS THE FIRST COMMANDMENT?

A. The first commandment is, 'Thou shalt have no other gods before me."

EXPLANATION:

The first commandment serves as the introduction, the gateway to the other nine because our obedience to them demonstrates that we serve the one true God and no other. The catechism helps us understand what God requires and what He forbids concerning each commandment.

Q46 | WHAT IS REQUIRED IN THE FIRST COMMANDMENT?

A. The first commandment requireth us to know and acknowledge God to be the only true God, and our God, and to worship and glorify Him accordingly.

Q47 | WHAT IS FORBIDDEN IN THE FIRST COMMANDMENT?

A.   The first commandment forbiddeth the denying, or not worshipping and glorifying the true God as God, and our God, and the giving of that worship and glory to any other which is due to Him alone.

EXPLANATION:

It's odd when people say that there is no God. These people call themselves atheists. They say they need more "evidence" of God's existence before they can believe. But Paul tells us that "His invisible attributes...have been clearly perceived, ever since the creation of the world, in the things that have been made. So they are without excuse" (Romans 1:20). It's a wonder that they can look outside on a beautiful fall afternoon, see the vibrant reds, oranges, yellows, greens, and browns against the backdrop of a blazing sun and a crystal-clear blue sky and not bow down and worship at the feet of our marvelous Creator! The problem is that their eyes are blind because they're dead spiritually. As Paul says, their thinking is futile and their hearts are darkened (Romans 1:21).

Even so, the Bible tells us there really are no atheists. Everyone worships something or someone! Those who reject God "exchange the truth about God for a lie and worship the creature rather than the Creator" (Romans 1:25). This false worship can take the form of all kinds of idols – statues and pictures of things we find in nature – or even the worship of other people, or other man-made religions. All of these are forbidden in the first commandment.

Q48 | WHAT ARE WE SPECIALLY TAUGHT BY THESE WORDS BEFORE ME IN THE FIRST COMMANDMENT?

A. These words, *before me* in the first commandment teach us, that God, who seeth all things, taketh notice of, and is much displeased with, the sin of having any other God.

EXPLANATION:

But for those of us who know the God of Scripture, how can we not acknowledge and worship the one, true God? For He is our Creator, the one who made us and all things. He is our Redeemer, the one who sent His Son to pay for our sins so and sent His Spirit so that we might have eternal life in His name. And He is our Provider, the One who "feeds the hungry" (Psalm 146:7) and directs our lives for our good and His glory (Romans 8:28). He alone is our God, and we must worship and glorify Him!

CHALLENGE QUESTIONS:

- What does David say about the person who says there is no God (Psalm 14:1)?

- What evidence does God give that He exists (Psalm 19:1)?

- Name some things that God has done that make you want to worship Him.

PRAYER:

"Oh come, let us worship and bow down; let us kneel before the LORD, our Maker! For he is our God, and we are the people of his pasture, and the sheep of his hand" (Psalm 95:6-7). *Gracious God, help us to worship You alone and to give You the glory for the great things You have done for us. In Jesus name we pray, Amen.*

SHORTER CATECHISM
QUESTIONS 49-52

Q49 | WHICH IS THE SECOND COMMANDMENT?

A. The second commandment is, *Thou shalt not make unto thee any graven image, or any likeness of any thing that is in heaven above, or that is in the earth beneath, or that is in the water under the earth; thou shalt not bow down thyself to them, nor serve them: for I the LORD thy God am a jealous God, visiting the iniquity of the fathers upon the children unto the third and fourth generation of them that hate me; and shewing mercy unto thousands of those that love me, and keep my commandments.*

EXPLANATION:

If you remember from our last study, we talked about idols or images that people worship in place of the one true God. As we look at the Old Testament, we see that this is a problem not only for the Gentiles who didn't profess faith in the Lord, but also for the Israelites who did. How can we forget what happened when Moses received the ten commandments on Mt. Sinai and God's people, led by Aaron, the High Priest, crafted and then worshiped a golden calf. This is something that God does not allow, and the people are punished for it as twenty-three thousand die in one day (1 Corinthians 10:8)! The catechism gives us the reasons why:

Q52 | WHAT ARE THE REASONS ANNEXED TO THE SECOND COMMANDMENT?

A.   The reasons annexed to the second commandment are, God's sovereignty over us, His propriety in us, and the zeal He hath to His own worship.

EXPLANATION:

In other words, "God totally rules over us, we belong to Him, and He is eager to be worshiped correctly."[18] So He gives us the second commandment to show us how we are to worship Him.

Q50 | WHAT IS REQUIRED IN THE SECOND COMMANDMENT?

A.   The second commandment requireth the receiving, observing, and keeping pure and entire, all such religious worship and ordinances as God hath appointed in His Word.

---

18 Douglas Kelly and Philip Rollinson, *The Shorter Catechism in Modern English* (Presbyterian and Reformed Publishing Company, Phillipsburg, NJ) 1986, p. 52.

When you look at your church bulletin, what do you see? Hopefully there's a clear order of worship that includes the activities (or elements) of worship that God has commanded: the singing of "psalms, and hymns, and spiritual songs" (Ephesians 5:19); the lifting up of "supplications, prayers, intercessions, and thanksgivings" (1 Timothy 2:1); the public reading and preaching of Scripture (1 Timothy 4:13); the Lord's Supper (1 Corinthians 11:26) and baptism (Matthew 28:19). When we worship according to God's Word, we please Him and bring glory to His name. So what should we avoid in worship?

Q51 | WHAT IS FORBIDDEN IN THE SECOND COMMANDMENT?

A.   The second commandment forbiddeth the worshiping of God by images, or any other way not appointed in His Word.

EXPLANATION:

We see here that we're not to make up new ways to worship that He hasn't commanded. We're also to avoid worshiping Him using images, either of false gods or of the one true God. We're forbidden to create images (pictures, statutes, etc.) to represent any Person of the Trinity and to worship them. Moses reminds us of this in Deuteronomy:

"Therefore watch yourselves very carefully. Since you saw no form on the day that the LORD spoke to you at Horeb out of the midst of the fire, beware lest you act corruptly by making a carved image for yourselves, in the form of any figure....(and) you be drawn away and bow down to them and serve them" (Deuteronomy 4:15-19).

Let us then worship according to God's Word, "in reverence and in awe for our God is a consuming fire" (Hebrews 12:28-29).

CHALLENGE QUESTIONS:

- Can you think of some times in the Old Testament when God's people worshiped idols?

- What are some things that Paul calls idols in the New Testament (Colossians. 3:5)?

- What are some other "idols of the heart" you can identify?

PRAYER:

Heavenly Father, may we worship You in Spirit and in truth. Forgive us for worshiping idols. Help us to worship You from the heart and according to Your Word.

53-56

SHORTER CATECHISM
QUESTIONS 53-56

Q53 | WHICH IS THE THIRD COMMANDMENT?

A. The third commandment is, Thou shalt not take the name of the LORD thy God in vain: for the LORD will not hold him guiltless that taketh his name in vain.

EXPLANATION:

Sadly, it's not uncommon for us to hear people using God's name in ways He never intended. In normal conversation, as well as on radio, shows we stream, books and magazines, people take the many wonderful names of God in vain, which means to take them lightly. They don't consider the majesty and glory of His name. Sometimes, they use them as curse words when they're angry at something or someone. Others shout them out as exclamations when they're happy. Still others do so in a popular acronym to emphasis texts or social media posts. All of these grieve our Heavenly Father deeply because they are not setting apart His name as holy. This is forbidden in the third commandment:

Q54 | WHAT IS REQUIRED IN THE THIRD COMMANDMENT?

A. The third commandment requireth the holy and reverent use of God's names, titles, attributes, ordinances, Word, and works.

Q55 | WHAT IS FORBIDDEN IN THE THIRD COMMANDMENT?

A. The third commandment forbiddeth all profaning or abusing of anything whereby God maketh himself known.

EXPLANATION:

Instead of using God's names, titles, and attributes (those things that describe the Triune God) in ugly, sinful ways, we're to use them to call upon Him in prayer, in praise, and in encouraging one another to love and worship Him. King David sets a great example in this marvelous prayer near the end of his life:

> "Blessed are you, O LORD, the God of Israel our father, forever and ever. Yours, O LORD, is the greatness and the power and the glory and the victory and the majesty, for all that is in the heavens and in the earth is yours. Yours is the kingdom, O LORD, and you are exalted as head above all....And now we thank you, our God, and praise your glorious name" (1 Chronicles 29:10-13).

And it's not just His name, titles, and attributes, we're also to make good use of His ordinances, those things that He's ordained for us to do in worship (Acts 2:42). We're to make sure that when we come into the sanctuary on Sundays, we're not just drawing near to God with our lips, but also with our hearts (Isaiah 29:13). The same is true with His Word. We're not merely to be hearers, but also doers of the Word (James 1:22). Otherwise, we're not honoring His name. How about His works? As we've seen throughout the catechism, God reveals Himself in the works of creation, redemption, and providence. If we're to keep the third commandment, we're to speak about His mighty works to one another (Psalm 145:4) and to proclaim His work of salvation through Jesus Christ to the lost (Romans 10:14-17).

It's tragic that so many take our Sovereign God lightly, abusing and profaning His name. But He does take notice. The answer to Question 56 reminds us of this truth:

Q56 | WHAT IS THE REASON ANNEXED TO THE THIRD COMMANDMENT?

A. The reason annexed to the third commandment is that, however the breakers of this commandment may escape punishment from men, yet the Lord our God will not suffer them to escape his righteous judgment.

EXPLANATION:

As believers in the Triune God, let us "continually offer up a sacrifice of praise to God, that is, the fruit of lips that acknowledge His name" (Hebrews 13:15).

CHALLENGE QUESTIONS:

- Where are some places you hear God's name taken in vain?

- When are times you're tempted to do so?

- Name some positive ways to keep the third commandment.

PRAYER:

"Worthy are you, our Lord and God, to receive glory and honor and power, for you created all things and by your will they existed and were created" (Revelation 4:11). Forgive us for taking your name in vain. Purify our lips so that they always praise you. In Jesus' name, Amen.

SHORTER CATECHISM
QUESTIONS 57-59

Q57 | WHICH IS THE FOURTH COMMANDMENT?

A. The fourth commandment is, *Remember the Sabbath day, to keep it holy. Six days shalt thou labour, and do all thy work: but the seventh day is the Sabbath of the LORD thy God: in it thou shalt not do any work, thou, nor thy son, nor thy daughter, nor thy manservant, nor thy maidservant, nor thy cattle, nor thy stranger that is within thy gates: for in six days the LORD made heaven and earth, the sea, and all that in them is, and rested the seventh day: wherefore the LORD blessed the sabbath day, and hallowed it.*

EXPLANATION:

Last time, we talked about using the Lord's name in a holy way. Now, we see we're to use the Lord's Day in a holy manner. You see, the Lord gave us a gift right after creating the heavens and the earth and everything in them. He did all of that in six days. But He rested on the seventh day – not because He was tired – but so that He might admire His glorious work and set an example for us to do the same. By doing so, He blessed it and made it holy. He set it apart so that we too might rest from our normal work and activities. He gives us this Sabbath Day each week to think about Him, to worship Him, and to enjoy His beautiful creation. Since this day is the most special day in our lives, the catechism has lots to say about it.

Q58 | WHAT IS REQUIRED IN THE FOURTH COMMANDMENT?

A. The fourth commandment requireth the keeping holy to God such set times as he hath appointed in his Word; expressly one whole day in seven, to be a holy Sabbath to himself.

EXPLANATION:

During the Old Testament days, God's people were to rest and worship on the seventh day, our Saturday. This is what the Lord modeled for us during the creation week. If you read through the book of Leviticus, you notice that there are lots of other sabbaths and feast days commanded for the Israelites. However, the center of their worship was the weekly sabbath. The same is true for us today, but something has changed!

Q59 | WHICH DAY OF THE SEVEN HATH GOD APPOINTED TO BE THE WEEKLY SABBATH?

A. From the beginning of the world to the resurrection of Christ, God appointed the seventh day of the week to be the weekly Sabbath; and the first day of the week ever since, to continue to the end of the world, which is the Christian Sabbath.

EXPLANATION:

That's right! Jesus, the Lord of the Sabbath (Mark 2:27-28), rose again from the dead on the first day of the week. Just as God crowned the creation week with a day of rest, our Lord Jesus crowned the first day of the week by finishing His work of salvation by rising from the dead! We now call Sunday the "Christian Sabbath" or the Lord's Day (Revelation 1:10). And we see that very early in the life of the church, God's people met on the first day of the week for worship (John 20:19; 1 Corinthians 16:1-2; Acts 20:7).

And the good news for Christians is this. Every time we rest and worship on the Lord's Day, God gives us a taste of our eternal rest in heaven as we meet with Jesus and enjoy sweet fellowship with His people. As the writer of Hebrews tells us, "So then, there remains a Sabbath rest for the people of God" (Hebrews 4:9).

Let's thank the Lord for His gracious gift of Sabbath rest each week by setting apart the Lord's Day for worship and for rest.

CHALLENGE QUESTIONS:

- What would you say to someone who thinks that we shouldn't keep the fourth commandment anymore?

- Why do we worship on Sunday instead of Saturday?

PRAYER:

Lord of the Sabbath, we pray that you would give us grace to set apart the Lord's Day for worship and rest. These things we ask in your name, Amen.

SHORTER CATECHISM
QUESTIONS 60-62

Q60 | HOW IS THE SABBATH TO BE SANCTIFIED?

A. The Sabbath is to be sanctified by a holy resting all that day, even from such worldly employments and recreations as are lawful on other days; and spending the whole time in the public and private exercises of God's worship, except so much as is to be taken up in the works of necessity and mercy.

EXPLANATION:

In our second look at the fourth commandment, the Catechism teaches us how to observe the Lord's Day; we're to rest throughout the day from our normal work and play. The Lord's Day is to be holy, set apart, different, distinct from all the others. God gives us this precious time to enjoy worshiping Him in public as we meet together as His people (Hebrews 10:25). This is something we must not neglect if we're to keep the fourth commandment! On the Lord's Day, we're also to worship Him at home, seeking Him in Scripture, prayer, and fellowship with our families and other believers. Sundays are also excellent times to read Christian books, magazines, and other Christian writings. In addition, Jesus, the Lord of the Sabbath, makes it clear that we're allowed to do works of necessity, like His disciples who picked grain on the Sabbath when hungry (Matthew 12:1-8). He also encourages works of mercy, like the many times He healed on the Sabbath (Matthew 12:9-13; Luke 13:10-17; 14:1-6; John 5:7). Works of necessity today include preparing food, opening and closing the church building, and serving as a first responder to keep communities safe. Works of mercy include delivering meals to shut-ins, working in the medical field, or helping a friend who is in distress.

Q61 | WHAT IS FORBIDDEN IN THE FOURTH COMMANDMENT?

A. The fourth commandment forbiddeth the omission, or careless performance, of the duties required, and the profaning the day by idleness, or doing that which is in itself sinful, or by unnecessary thoughts, words, or works, about our worldly employments or recreations.

EXPLANATION:

Wow! There's certainly a lot for us to think about when it comes to the way that we spend our Sundays! Our Lord wants us to be actively involved in worship, along with works of necessity and mercy. He doesn't want us to waste this wonderful weekly gift by being lazy, sinful, or distracted by thinking about or getting involved in our normal, daily routines. Instead, He wants us to rest so that we can be filled with the blessings that are ours through Jesus Christ:

> "If you turn back your foot from the Sabbath, from doing your pleasure on my holy day, and call the Sabbath a delight and the holy day of the LORD honorable; if you honor it, not going your own ways, or seeking your own pleasure, or talking idly; then you shall take delight in the LORD, and I will make you ride on the heights of the earth; I will feed you with the heritage of Jacob your father, for the mouth of the LORD has spoken" (Isaiah 58:13-14).

Q62 | WHAT ARE THE REASONS ANNEXED TO THE FOURTH COMMANDMENT?

A. The reasons annexed to the fourth commandment are, God's allowing us six days of the week for our own employments, his challenging a special propriety in the seventh, his own example, and his blessing the Sabbath-day.

EXPLANATION:

Even though our Lord has blessed the Sabbath Day and called it holy, many of us get frustrated that we can't do what we want on the Lord's Day. We want to use it as a day to sleep in, to catch up on school or other work, to shop, or even for binging sports and movies. Yet what did our Lord tell us? We have six days for all those other activities. Let's use those days wisely so that we can fully enjoy God's holy day of rest!

CHALLENGE QUESTIONS:

- What activities help us to keep the Lord's Day in a holy manner?
- What activities prevent us from keeping it holy?
- How should we order our week so that we're free to worship and rest on Sundays?

PRAYER:

Lord of the Sabbath, you have told us that the Sabbath was made for man, and not man for the Sabbath (Mark 2:27). Forgive us when we've failed to keep your Day holy. Help us instead "to rejoice and be glad in your special day"(Psalm 118:24). In Jesus' name we pray, Amen.

SHORTER CATECHISM
QUESTIONS 63-66

Q63 | WHICH IS THE FIFTH COMMANDMENT?

A. The fifth commandment is, *Honor thy father and thy mother: that thy days may be long upon the land which the* **LORD** *thy God giveth thee.*

EXPLANATION:

"Beloved, let us love one another, for love is from God, and whoever loves has been born of God and knows God" (1 John 4:7). These words from the Apostle John are a good introduction to the last six commandments which show us how to love our neighbor. The fifth commandment speaks about our relationships, starting with family life. Children are commanded to honor their fathers and mothers. This means to love, respect, and obey parents because it is right and pleasing to the Lord (Ephesians 6:1; Colossians 3:20). But this commandment impacts all our relationships.

127

Q64 | WHAT IS REQUIRED IN THE FIFTH COMMANDMENT?

A. The fifth commandment requireth the preserving the honor and performing the duties, belonging to everyone in their several places and relations, as superiors, inferiors, or equals.

EXPLANATION:

Now, all of that may sound confusing at first, but it's quite simple. If we're a "superior," like a parent, teacher, employer, community or church leader, we're to honor and work for the good of those under our care. As Paul writes to fathers, "do not provoke your children to anger, but bring them up in the discipline and instruction of the Lord" (Eph. 6:4). The same is true if we're an "inferior," those underneath the authority of someone else, whether in the workplace, school, home, church, or citizens under local, state, and national governments. As Romans 13:7 instructs us, we're to: "Pay to all what is owed to them: taxes to whom taxes are owed, revenue to whom revenue is owed, respect to whom respect is owed, honor to whom honor is owed."

We're also encouraged here to honor and respect our "equals," our peers, those who are in the same life situation. Peter summarizes this commandment beautifully: "Honor everyone. Love the brotherhood. Fear God. Honor the emperor" (1 Peter 2:17).

Q65 | WHAT IS FORBIDDEN IN THE FIFTH COMMANDMENT?

A. The fifth commandment forbiddeth the neglecting of, or doing anything against, the honor and duty which belongeth to everyone in their several places and relations.

EXPLANATION:

If we fail to honor, love, and serve others made in God's image, regardless of our relationship to them, we break the fifth commandment. Yet, the Lord gives us a promise if we do obey it!

Q66 | WHAT IS THE REASON ANNEXED TO THE FIFTH COMMANDMENT?

A. The reason annexed to the fifth commandment is, a promise of long life and prosperity (as far as it shall serve for God's glory and their own good) to all such as keep this commandment.

EXPLANATION:

What a promise of blessing! Sometimes, to serve God's glory and our own good, He withholds these, but generally speaking, those who honor their parents, and all relationships, enjoy long life and prosperity. And even if these aren't experienced physically, all who are in Christ Jesus experience abundant, eternal, fruit-filled life when walk in His commandments (John 15:1-17).

CHALLENGE QUESTIONS:

- How can learning to love our parents and teachers help us learn to love and respect God?

- Name some ways that we typically break the fifth commandment. What is the blessing God promises to those who honor their parents?

PRAYER:

Heavenly Father, thank you for those whom you've placed in authority over us. Help us to honor them and all people. Forgive us when we've failed to do so. Help us to bear fruit as we abide in you by keeping your commandments. In Jesus' name we pray, Amen.

SHORTER CATECHISM
QUESTIONS 67-69

Q67 | WHICH IS THE SIXTH COMMANDMENT?

A.   The sixth commandment is, *Thou shalt not kill.*

EXPLANATION:

It's really tempting when we read this commandment to think: "Well, I don't have to worry about this one too much. I've never killed anybody and I'm not planning on killing anyone. Finally, a commandment I can keep!" But there is much more to keeping the sixth commandment than meets the eye! Let's begin by looking at what the sixth commandment requires:

Q68 | WHAT IS REQUIRED IN THE SIXTH COMMANDMENT?

A.   The sixth commandment requireth all lawful endeavors to preserve our own life, and the life of others.

EXPLANATION:

One way we preserve our own lives is by leading a healthy lifestyle: eating nutritious foods, exercising our bodies, and getting enough sleep each night. Obeying this command would also include providing clothing and shelter for ourselves and for our families, in addition to acting in self-defense when attacked. We also should work to preserve the lives of others by coming to their aid in times of danger and need. And when we're unable to help by ourselves, we seek aid from the church and from local authorities, depending upon the circumstances.

Also, instead of speaking, thinking, or acting out of hatred and violence, we must, "turn away from evil and do good; seek peace and pursue it" (Psalm 34:14). Rather than seeking harm, even against our enemies, we should pray for them and work for their good. We know that this is impossible in our strength, but we serve a Savior who "opened not His mouth" (Isaiah 53:7) in vengeance, but prayed for those who crucified Him, pleading "Father, forgive them, for they know not what they do" (Luke 23:34).

Q69 | WHAT IS FORBIDDEN IN THE SIXTH COMMANDMENT?

A.   The sixth commandment forbiddeth the taking away of our own life, or the life of our neighbor unjustly, or whatsoever tendeth thereunto.

EXPLANATION:

It's clear from the Bible that we're not to commit suicide or even to engage in risky behaviors that might lead to our death. The Larger Catechism also mentions things like eating too much, drinking alcohol to excess, and the abusing of drugs, whether illegal or prescription. It also speaks about working too hard and playing too hard, not allowing enough time for rest (see LC 135,136). Of course, we're also not to take the life of our neighbor without a right cause. Right causes include times of warfare, self-defense, and the death penalty that our justice system carries out for certain crimes.

But the fifth commandment speaks not just to what we do; we're also to be careful about what we say and of what's lurking inside of our hearts. As our Lord preaches in the Sermon on the Mount:

> "You have heard that it was said to those of old, 'You shall not murder; and whoever murders will be liable to judgment.' But I say to you that everyone who is angry with his brother will be liable to judgment; whoever insults his brother will be liable to the council; and whoever says, 'You fool!' will be liable to the hell of fire" (Matthew 5:21-22).

In other words, when we think angry, hateful, violent thoughts about others or say cruel things that tear them down, we're breaking the sixth commandment.

CHALLENGE QUESTIONS:

- Name some ways we can help to preserve our own lives. How can we preserve the lives of others?

- What are some ways we break the sixth commandment in our thoughts?

- In our words?

- In our actions?

PRAYER:

Gracious Heavenly Father, "so far as it depends on us, let us live peaceably with all" (Romans 12:18). Forgive us for our angry thoughts, words, and actions. Help us to take care of ourselves, our families, and our neighbors. In Jesus' name we pray, Amen.

70-72

SHORTER CATECHISM
QUESTIONS 70-72

Q70 | WHICH IS THE SEVENTH COMMANDMENT?

A. **The seventh commandment is,** *Thou shalt not commit adultery.*

EXPLANATION:

When we hear the word adultery, we think of an act of unfaithfulness within a marriage. As the writer of Hebrews tells us:

> "Let marriage be held in honor among all, and let the marriage bed be undefiled, for God will judge the sexually immoral and adulterous" (Hebrews 13:4).

However, the seventh commandment also speaks to those who are unmarried too, including children and young people. Like all of God's commandments, keeping it requires more than doing the right thing. It also speaks to our thoughts and words.

Q71 | WHAT IS REQUIRED IN THE SEVENTH COMMANDMENT?

A.   The seventh commandment requireth the preservation of our own, and our neighbor's chastity, in heart, speech, and behaviour.

Q72 | WHAT IS FORBIDDEN IN THE SEVENTH COMMANDMENT?

A.   The seventh commandment forbiddeth all unchaste thoughts, words, and actions.

EXPLANATION:

Chastity is a word we don't hear very often in today's world, but it means modesty, purity, or virtue in ourselves and in our relationships with others. Sadly, chastity isn't valued or praised in our culture today. But the Bible tells us that we're to "flee from sexual immorality" because our bodies are "temples of the Holy Spirit." Therefore, we're to "glorify God in our bodies" (1 Corinthians 6:19-20). The same is true concerning our speech: "Let there be no filthiness nor foolish talk nor crude joking, which are out of place, but instead let there be thanksgiving" (Ephesians 5:4).

Jesus also commands that we keep our hearts pure, too: "You have heard that it was said, 'You shall not commit adultery.' But I say to you that everyone who looks at a woman with lustful intent has already committed adultery with her in his heart" (Matthew 5:27-28).

Like Job, we must "make a covenant with our eyes" (Job 31:1) so that we treat all whom we meet with dignity and respect, not as mere objects of our sinful appetites and desires. The same is true for what we see on the internet, in magazines, and in movies. We must avoid pornography in any form and turn away from its use immediately. We must guard our hearts, putting to death "what is earthly in us: sexual immorality, impurity, passion, evil desire, and covetousness, which is idolatry" (Colossians 3:5). Instead, we need to pray for the Holy Spirit's help to "put on as God's chosen ones, holy and beloved, compassionate hearts, kindness, humility, meekness, and patience" (Colossians 3:12).

Now, if you've broken this commandment in any way, do not despair. There is great hope for you in Christ if you come to Him and turn away from your sin! As Paul encourages us in 1 Corinthians:

> "Do not be deceived: neither the sexually immoral, nor idolaters, nor adulterers, nor men who practice homosexuality, nor thieves, nor the greedy, nor drunkards, nor revilers, nor swindlers will inherit the kingdom of God. And such *were* some of you. But you were *washed*, you were *sanctified*, you were *justified* in the name of the Lord Jesus Christ and by the Spirit of our God" (1 Corinthians 6:9-11).

CHALLENGE QUESTIONS:

- Which sins are covered under the seventh commandment in addition to marital unfaithfulness?

- Name some challenges to remaining sexually pure in our culture today.

PRAYER:

Heavenly Father, may "sexual immorality and all impurity or covetousness not even be named among us, as is proper among saints" (Ephesians 5:3). Forgive us when we've broken the seventh commandment. And now, keep us pure in heart, word, and conduct. In Jesus' name, Amen.

SHORTER CATECHISM
QUESTIONS 73-75

Q73 | WHICH IS THE EIGHTH COMMANDMENT?

A.   The eighth commandment is, *Thou shalt not steal.*

EXPLANATION:

We all understand what it means to steal. It means taking or using something that doesn't belong to us. Because our Lord is gracious, instead of stealing, He calls us to trust that He will supply our daily bread – all our daily needs (Matthew 6:11). Aren't you thankful that we don't serve a stingy God? Though "the earth is the Lord's and the fullness thereof" (Psalm 24:1), He generously blesses us with all manner of good and perfect gifts (James 1:17), including money and possessions. And the eighth commandment not only prohibits us from stealing, but also encourages us to be good stewards of God's physical blessings.

Q74 | WHAT IS REQUIRED IN THE EIGHTH COMMANDMENT?

A. The eighth commandment requireth the lawful procuring and furthering the wealth and outward estate of ourselves and others.

EXPLANATION:

Remember our discussion of the fourth commandment? The Lord tells us, "Six days shalt thou labor and do all thy work" (Exodus 20:9). God expects us to work hard during the week so that we can provide for ourselves and our families. This is true for men (Genesis 2:15) and women (Proverbs 31:10-17), whether working outside the home or within. Instead of lazily despising our work we should consider it a calling from our gracious God. As Paul writes, we should labor,

> "...with sincerity of heart, fearing the Lord. Whatever you do, work heartily, as for the Lord and not for men, knowing that from the Lord you will receive the inheritance as your reward. You are serving the Lord Christ" (Colossians 3:22-24).

Working hard for our Lord Jesus Christ is one lawful way to obtain and build wealth. So is receiving an inheritance from parents or other loved ones. What is important to remember, though, is that we're not to hoard our wealth. We're to give generously to the church so that we do not "rob God" (Malachi 3:8-12). Instead, we're to "lay up treasures in heaven" (Matthew 6:20). And as the Lord blesses, we're to use His gifts to bless others, especially those in need. We're to "look after the interests of others" (Philippians 2:4), especially "those who are of the household of faith" (Galatians 6:9-10), our brothers and sisters in Christ.

> ## Q75 | WHAT IS FORBIDDEN IN THE EIGHTH COMMANDMENT?
>
> **A.** The eighth commandment forbiddeth whatsoever doth, or may, unjustly hinder our own, or our neighbor's wealth or outward estate.

EXPLANATION:

The eighth commandment instructs us not to steal from anyone else. This is certainly true concerning money and possessions. But there are other ways we can be guilty of stealing. We can steal time from our employers by not giving our best effort, talking too much with coworkers, or browsing the internet on company time. We can steal ideas by plagiarizing papers or cheating on tests. We can steal credit on projects by failing to acknowledge help from other individuals. We can steal from our own households by failing to work (1 Timothy 5:18), falling into debt (Proverbs 22:7), or making risky investments.

Paul sums up this commandment well:

"Let the thief no longer steal, but rather let him labor, doing honest work with his own hands, so that he may have something to share with anyone in need" (Ephesians 4:28).

CHALLENGE QUESTIONS:

- Name some lawful ways to build wealth. What are some unlawful ways?

- How does taking care of those in need reflect God's character?

PRAYER:

Heavenly Father, help us to be honest and hard-working as we serve you. Give us generous hearts. May we "not grow weary of doing good, for in due season we will reap if we do not give up" (Galatians 6:9). In Jesus' name, Amen.

SHORTER CATECHISM
QUESTIONS 76-78

Q76 | WHICH IS THE NINTH COMMANDMENT?

A.   The ninth commandment is, *Thou shalt not bear false witness against thy neighbor.*

EXPLANATION:

When you think about bearing witness, what comes to mind? Do you imagine placing your hand on a Bible in a courtroom, swearing to tell "the truth, the whole truth, and nothing but the truth?" Well, telling the truth is at the heart of the ninth commandment. This is certainly true when we've taken a special oath as a witness in a legal matter. As Solomon reminds us: "A faithful witness does not lie, but a false witness breathes out lies...A truthful witness saves lives, but one who breathes out lies is deceitful" (Proverbs 14:5, 25).

But we're not just to tell the truth when we're under oath, we're to be honest with everyone, including our family members, teachers, and friends.

Q77 | WHAT IS REQUIRED IN THE NINTH COMMANDMENT?

A. The ninth commandment requireth the maintaining and promoting of truth between man and man, and of our own and our neighbor's good name, especially in witness-bearing.

Q78 | WHAT IS FORBIDDEN IN THE NINTH COMMANDMENT?

A. The ninth commandment forbiddeth whatsoever is prejudicial to truth, or injurious to our own, or our neighbor's good name.

EXPLANATION:

There are many places in Scripture where we're told to tell the truth and not to lie. Here are two examples:

"Speak the truth to one another; render in your gates judgments that are true and make for peace; do not devise evil in your hearts against one another, and love no false oath, for all these things I hate, declares the LORD" (Zechariah 8:16-17).

"Therefore, having put away falsehood, let each one of you speak the truth with his neighbor, for we are members one of another" (Ephesians 4:25).

You see, by telling the truth, we reflect the very character of God, for "it is impossible for God to lie" (Hebrews 6:18) and "the words of the LORD are pure words, like silver refined in a furnace on the ground, purified seven times" (Psalm 12:6).

The catechism also encourages us to "maintain and promote" our own good name. We do this by seeking to think, say, and do what is right. As the Psalmist tells us:

"He who walks blamelessly and does what is right and speaks truth in his heart; who does not slander with his tongue and does no evil to his neighbor, nor takes up a reproach against his friend" (Psalm 15:2-3).

Though we'll never be perfect, we achieve a good name if we're growing in these things, becoming more and more like Jesus every day! And when we fall short, we ask for God's and our neighbor's forgiveness. We also work to clear our name and preserve the good name of others when false accusations fly. Above all, we don't participate in gossip, whispering in private, or slander, ruining someone's reputation in public. Not only are we forbidden from spreading lies and rumors, but we're also forbidden from using the truth as a weapon, unnecessarily repeating secrets, or other information that will harm another person. Instead, we're to "speak the truth in love" using our speech to praise God and to build one another up (Ephesians 4:15, 29).

CHALLENGE QUESTIONS:

- Is it okay to tell "little white lies?"
- Why is it important to have a good name?
- How should we respond when we hear gossip or slander?

PRAYER:

Heavenly Father, may our speech always be "gracious, seasoned with salt" (Colossians 4:6). In love, may we always rejoice in truth and reject lies (1 Corinthians 13:6). In Jesus' name, Amen.

SHORTER CATECHISM
QUESTIONS 79-81

Q79 | WHICH IS THE TENTH COMMANDMENT?

A.   The tenth commandment is *Thou shalt not covet thy neighbor's house, thou shalt not covet thy neighbor's wife, nor his man-servant, nor his maid-servant, nor his ox, nor his donkey, nor anything that is thy neighbor's.*

Q80 | WHAT IS REQUIRED IN THE TENTH COMMANDMENT?

A.   The tenth commandment requireth the full contentment with our own condition, with a right and charitable frame of spirit toward our neighbor; and all that is his.

EXPLANATION:

At Christmas children love to make their lists and then dream about what might be under the tree. At a friend's birthday party, we might really struggle when they unwrap that present we've secretly wanted. The thing is, coveting – not being happy or satisfied with what we have and desiring more – doesn't stop once all the gifts have been unwrapped. Because of our sinful hearts, we constantly crave what belongs to others. And it's not just material possessions; we're capable of coveting anything that belongs to our neighbor! Remember the words of our Savior:

> "Take care, and be on your guard against all covetousness, for one's life does not consist in the abundance of his possessions" (Luke 12:15).

Yes. The tenth commandment stands out above the others because it's the one that's more easily "hidden." The other nine involve both "outward actions and inward desires." But the commandment not to covet is all about the heart. And coveting is often at the "root" of other sins, including Adam and Eve's eating the forbidden fruit in the garden.[19] James says this:

> "But each person is tempted when he is lured and enticed by his own desire. Then desire when it has conceived gives birth to sin, and sin when it is fully grown brings forth death" (James 1:14-15).

Paul even says that coveting is "idolatry" (Ephesians 5:5), putting things and people in the place of God and worshiping

---

19 GI Williamson, *The Westminster Shorter Catechism for Study Classes* (Presbyterian and Reformed Publishing: Phillipsburg, NJ), 2003, p. 272.

them. Therefore, it's important to guard our hearts against evil desires so that our coveting doesn't lead to sins against our neighbors like lying, stealing, committing adultery, or acting in violence. As the catechism instructs:

Q81 | WHAT IS FORBIDDEN IN THE TENTH COMMANDMENT?

A. **The tenth commandment forbiddeth all discontentment with our own estate, envying or grieving at the good of our neighbor, and all inordinate motions and affections to any thing that is his.**

EXPLANATION:

So what is the antidote to coveting? It's contentment! It's being thankful for what God, in His grace has given us spiritually in His Son Jesus Christ. It's enjoying our blessings in Christ and looking forward in hope to the "riches of His glorious inheritance" (Ephesians 1:3, 18). It's being satisfied with the physical blessings, our daily bread, the Father provides. The Apostle Paul says it best:

"I have learned in whatever situation I am to be content. I know how to be brought low, and I know how to abound. In any and every circumstance, I have learned the secret of facing plenty and hunger, abundance and need. I can do all things through him who strengthens me" (Philippians 4:11-13).

CHALLENGE QUESTIONS:

- Why is coveting often the root of other sins?
- Can you name some spiritual and physical blessings that you're thankful for?

PRAYER:

O Lord, "You have chosen our portion and cup. You hold our lot. The lines have fallen for us in pleasant places. We have a beautiful inheritance"(Psalm 16:5-6) in Christ. Make us thankful and content. In His name we pray, Amen.

SHORTER CATECHISM
QUESTION 82

Q82 | **IS ANY MAN ABLE PERFECTLY TO KEEP THE COMMANDMENTS OF GOD?**

A.   No mere man, since the fall, is able in this life perfectly to keep the commandments of God, but doth daily break them in thought, word, and deed.

EXPLANATION:

There's no feeling quite as wonderful as getting a test back with 100 written in red at the top – a perfect score! I can remember a certain teacher making smiley faces in the zeroes to make it that much more special. For most of us, it's rare to earn a perfect score in any activity we attempt. When it comes to God's law, no mere human being is even capable of it. Instead, because we are born into sin, we daily break the commandments in our thoughts, words, and actions. Of course, this is true for non-believers. It's also true for Christians. Consider these Scriptures:

"...the intention of man's heart is evil from his youth" (Genesis 8:21).

"...no human being can tame the tongue. It is a restless evil, full of deadly poison" (James 3:8).

"So I find it to be a law that when I want to do right, evil lies close at hand. For I delight in the law of God, in my inner being, but I see in my members another law waging war against the law of my mind and making me captive to the law of sin that dwells in my members" (Romans 7:21-23).

God's Word is clear: "...for all have sinned and fall short of the glory of God" (Romans 3:23).

However, there is one man who did keep the law perfectly for His people – our Lord Jesus Christ. He is no "mere man;" instead, He is the Son of God, the perfect God-man. And though He took on human flesh, was born of a woman, and obeyed the law that He Himself decreed, He lived a life of perfect obedience:

"For we do not have a high priest who is unable to sympathize with our weaknesses, but one who in every respect has been tempted as we are, yet without sin" (Hebrews 4:15).

"He humbled himself by becoming obedient to the point of death, even death on a cross" (Philippians 2:8).

That's right! Jesus made the 100 on the obedience test. And though we are guilty of breaking God's law, our Heavenly Father accepts His score on our behalf when we trust in Him and turn away from our sins. We'll have more to say about that in the devotions to follow.

At the same time, those who trust in Jesus are called to obey Him. We're to do so, not for our salvation, but out of love and gratitude. As Jesus tells His disciples, "If you love me, you will keep my commandments" (John 14:15). And though we are not saved *by* our good works (Romans 3:20), we are saved *for* them:

> "For we are his workmanship, created in Christ Jesus for good works, which God prepared beforehand, that we should walk in them" (Ephesians 2:10).

That's right! We've been born again. We have a new heart. We're new creations in Christ (2 Corinthians 5:17). And though we don't do so perfectly, the Holy Spirit enables us to walk in a way that is pleasing to Him (1 Thessalonians 4:1) as He transforms us more and more into the image of our Savior Jesus Christ (2 Corinthians 3:18).

CHALLENGE QUESTIONS:

- Which of the ten commandments are you having the hardest time obeying right now?

- Is it in your thoughts, words, or actions?

- What should we do when we're tempted to disobey (1 Corinthians 10:13)?

PRAYER:

Heavenly Father, forgive us for the ways that we've broken your laws today in our thoughts, words, and actions. Thank you that Jesus perfectly obeyed your laws for us. Send your Spirit so that we would obey you more and more in Christ's resurrection power. In Jesus' name we pray, Amen.

SHORTER CATECHISM
QUESTIONS 83 & 84

Q83 | ARE ALL TRANSGRESSIONS OF THE LAW EQUALLY HEINOUS?

A. Some sins in themselves, and by reason of several aggravations, are more heinous in the sight of God than others.

Q84 | WHAT DOTH EVERY SIN DESERVE?

A. Every sin deserveth God's wrath and curse, both in this life, and that which is to come.

EXPLANATION:

You probably don't hear the word "heinous" used much in today's world. It means something that is especially offensive, shocking, scandalous, or evil. When it comes to our sins, every one of them is heinous in the sight of God and deserve His wrath and curse. Consider these Scriptures:

"For all who rely on works of the law are under a curse; for it is written, "Cursed be everyone who does not abide by *all things* written in the Book of the Law, and do them" (Galatians 3:10).

"For whoever keeps the whole law but *fails in one point* has become guilty of all of it" (James 2:10).

As the catechism reminds us, our sins put us underneath God's judgment here on the earth and certainly for all eternity: "Let no one deceive you with empty words, for because of these things the wrath of God comes upon the sons of disobedience" (Eph. 5:6).

But though all sins are heinous before God and worthy of His judgment, they're not equally so. Some sins grieve and offend Him more than others.[20] This can be because of the nature of the particular sin. For instance, when we sin directly against the Triune God (Commandments 1-4), it's worse than when we sin against our neighbor (Commandments 5-10): "If someone sins against a man, God will mediate for him, but if someone sins against the LORD, who can intercede for him?" (1 Samuel 2:25). Also, though both are deserving of eternal death in hell, there is a difference in severity between sinful thoughts and sinful actions.

Also, if someone in authority sins, like a preacher, elder, deacon, teacher, parent or politician, their sin is aggravated because it leads others to disobey God (James 3:1). As our Lord Jesus warns:

---

20 Thomas Vincent, *The Shorter Catechism Explained from Scripture* (The Banner of Truth Trust: 3 Murrayfield R., Edinburgh) 1980, p. 219.

"Whoever causes one of these little ones who believe in me to sin, it would be better for him if a great millstone were hung around his neck and he were thrown into the sea" (Mark 9:42).

Another circumstance that aggravates our sin is how much we know about Jesus and the Bible. The more we know, the more accountable we are. Jesus says that the cities where He lived, preached, and performed miracles would receive greater judgments than even the notorious city of Sodom (Matthew 11:20-24) which was destroyed by fire and brimstone! Yet, as heinous as our sins may be, God's grace through Jesus Christ is greater than all of them! We'll talk more about that in the devotions ahead.

CHALLENGE QUESTIONS:

- What makes certain sins more heinous than others?
- Why is it worse for us to sin right after a worship service than on a random Tuesday morning?
- Name some other ways our sins are aggravated.

PRAYER:

Heavenly Father, we bless your name because you "pardon all our iniquity" through the blood of Jesus Christ (Psalm 103:3). We've sinned against you today. Forgive us through the blood of our Lord Jesus. In His name we pray, Amen.

SHORTER CATECHISM
QUESTION 85

Q85 | WHAT DOTH GOD REQUIRE OF US, THAT WE MAY ESCAPE HIS WRATH AND CURSE, DUE TO US FOR SIN?

A. To escape the wrath and curse of God, due to us for sin, God requireth of us faith in Jesus Christ, repentance unto life, with the diligent use of all the outward means whereby Christ communicateth to us the benefits of redemption.

EXPLANATION:

Have you ever felt like you were in a situation where you couldn't escape? Maybe you were ticking along half-way up the first hill of a roller coaster and you just wanted to get off before the big drop. Or you were panicking moments before giving a speech. Or you wanted to escape the "wrath" of your parents after making a bad grade or getting in trouble at school! You feel helpless when there's no escape – when there's no way out. Thankfully, when it comes to the punishment we deserve for our sins, God has made a way for us to escape – through His Son Jesus Christ!

If you remember from our earlier devotions, our Heavenly Father made a covenant of grace with His elect people, promising a Redeemer to come. In the fullness of time, God's own Son came to the earth and took on human flesh so that He might live, die, and rise again to rescue us from sin, death, and hell. And though our redemption is through God's free grace alone, He requires three things of us to receive it. The first two you've probably heard before. Our Savior speaks of them in His first sermon:

> "Jesus came into Galilee, proclaiming the gospel of God, and saying, 'The time is fulfilled, and the kingdom of God is at hand; repent and believe in the gospel'" (Mark 1:14-15).

Yes! The good news is that we can escape God's wrath and curse by repenting (turning away from our sins), and believing (trusting in Jesus Christ alone). We'll have more to say about each of these in the days to come. But the third requirement may catch us a little off guard.

The catechism says that God requires us to be diligent (heartfelt, earnest, consistent) as we participate in the outward means of grace, the activities that Jesus uses to fill us with the blessings of our salvation. Peter says it this way:

> "Therefore, brothers, be all the more diligent to confirm your calling and election, for if you practice these qualities, you will never fall" (2 Peter 1:10).

It's not that those who truly repent and believe in Christ can fall away from salvation. Instead, the evidence or proof of our calling and election is that we continue to seek Christ in His means of grace.

And this is also the way we grow as Christians – by faithfully attending worship, reading our Bibles, praying, and experiencing Christian fellowship. It's not that doing these things automatically makes us holy. But when we're hearing the Word preached, enjoying the sacraments of baptism and the Lord's Supper, singing God's praise, and joining our hearts together in prayer, the Holy Spirit works in us to make us more like Jesus.

CHALLENGE QUESTIONS:

- Can you remember a time you felt like you couldn't escape?
- What three things does God require for us to escape His judgment?
- Is it possible to be a Christian (to repent and believe) and not have a desire to worship?

PRAYER:

Thank you, Heavenly Father, for the grace to repent of our sins and to believe in Christ. May we be more and more diligent to meet with you in worship, to read the Bible, and to pray so that we can enjoy more of your blessings. In Jesus' name we pray, Amen.

SHORTER CATECHISM
QUESTION 86

Q86 | WHAT IS FAITH IN JESUS CHRIST?

A. Faith in Jesus Christ is a saving grace, whereby we receive and rest upon Him alone for salvation, as he is offered to us in the gospel.

EXPLANATION:

The morning I wrote this, a neighborhood dog ran our family's beloved fifteen-year-old cat up a tree so that he was about twenty feet from the ground. Even after the dog left, the cat wouldn't come down. I tried to coax him, but he wouldn't budge. He began to panic! I thought about calling the Fire Department, but before taking that drastic step, I found a 10-foot ladder and climbed up to see how close I could get to him. Not very close! But as my arms reached up to him, the cat started crawling down, clinging closely to the tree. Finally, he came within range, let me gather him in, and he rested on my shoulder as we made our way down to safety. You see, he didn't trust himself to get all the way down, but when he saw me (and the ladder!), he knew that I wouldn't let him go and that we'd make it safely to the ground. This incident, in some small way, shows us what faith in Jesus Christ is all about – no longer relying on ourselves or anyone else – but receiving and resting on Him alone for our salvation.

As the catechism tells us, faith in Jesus Christ is a saving *grace*. It's a gift from God, not a work that earns His favor. Paul explains:

> "For by *grace* you have been saved through faith. And this is not your own doing; it is the gift of God, not a result of works, so that no one may boast" (Ephesians 2:8-9).

Naturally, because we were born into sin, we can't believe in Jesus Christ on our own. We might know who He is, as much of the world does. We might think that what the Bible says about Him is true – but "even the demons believe – and shudder (James 2:19). But it's not until the Holy Spirit causes us to be born again that we see our need for a Savior and are willing to put our trust in Him alone. As John writes:

> "But to all who did receive him, who believed in his name, he gave the right to become children of God, who were born, not of blood nor of the will of the flesh nor of the will of man, but of God" (John 1:12-13).

Keep something in mind. Faith, by itself, doesn't save us. Christ does. Faith is the instrument or the bridge that connects us to Christ. He is the object of our Faith revealed in the gospel, the good news. And what is this good news we must believe? It is that Jesus Christ, our Redeemer, lived a perfect life to give us His righteousness, died in our place to pay for our sins, and rose again so that we may enjoy eternal life through Him now and forever.

Are you like my old cat? Afraid and fully aware that you can't save yourself? If so, hear the good news and believe it! There is One who will never let you go and will lead you safely home to your Father's house.

> "And there is salvation in no one else, for there is no other name under heaven given among men by which we must be saved" (Acts 4:12).

His name is Jesus. Receive God's gracious gift of His Son and rest on Him alone for your salvation!

CHALLENGE QUESTIONS:

- Have you ever been stuck in a tree?
- Did you have to trust someone else to get down?
- What do you know about Jesus?
- Do you believe that what the Bible says about Him is true?
- Why can we trust Him to save us?

PRAYER:

Heavenly Father, may we believe the gospel – that "Jesus Christ is the Son of God. May we have faith in Him so that we have life in His name" (John 20:30-31). It is in His name we pray, Amen.

SHORTER CATECHISM
QUESTION 87

Q87 | WHAT IS REPENTANCE UNTO LIFE?

A. Repentance unto life is a saving grace, whereby a sinner, out of a true sense of his sin, and apprehension of the mercy of God in Christ, doth, with grief and hatred of sin, turn from it unto God, with full purpose of, and endeavor after, new obedience.

EXPLANATION:

Have you ever watched a marching band at halftime of a football game? Then chances are you've seen an about face. A line of marchers will be going one way; then, all of a sudden, they will turn around and start marching in the opposite direction. Now, if everyone's not in step with the music, the results of an about-face can be pretty comical. I once knocked the hat off the marcher in front of me with the slide of my trombone! But an about-face, properly executed, is a wonderful picture of repentance – turning 180 degrees away from our sin and walking in a new direction, toward Jesus our Lord.

Just as we saw with faith, repentance is a saving grace, a gift from God that leads to eternal life. We need to remember that faith and repentance always go together. We often say that they are two sides of the same coin. When we're born again by the Holy Spirit, we receive salvation by trusting in Christ, but also by turning away from our sins. When we come to Jesus for the first time in faith and repentance, we call that conversion. This is when we are justified in God's sight. But all true Christians continue to believe and to repent throughout their lives.

So what does repentance look like? First, it means more than saying "I'm sorry." Yes, it involves confessing our sins, but it's more than that. It's being bothered or convicted by sins so that we "grieve and hate" them. It's having a "true sense" of our sins – how they offend God, how they hurt others and even ourselves. However, when we repent, though we're saddened by our sins, we're not without hope! Because we understand God's mercy – His grace and love for us – in Jesus Christ. We understand that "if we confess our sins, God is faithful and just to forgive us our sins and to cleanse us from all unrighteousness" through the "blood of Jesus His Son" (1 John 1:7-9). Isn't that wonderful news? And His mercy is there for us even when we commit the worst sins imaginable. Consider David's words after committing adultery with Bathsheba and murdering her husband Uriah:

> "Have mercy on me, O God, according to your steadfast love; according to your abundant mercy blot out my transgressions. Wash me thoroughly from my iniquity, and cleanse me from my sin! For I know my transgressions, and my sin is ever before me. Against you, you only, have I sinned and done what is evil in your sight, so that you

may be justified in your words and blameless in your judgment" (Ps. 51:1-4).

Notice, too, from the catechism that repentance is more than words. It involves action. We turn to God "with full purpose of, and endeavor after, new obedience." We "bear fruit in keeping with repentance" (Matthew 3:8). Though we never do this perfectly, we set our hearts to think, feel, say, and do what is right in God's sight. To sum it up, instead of following the world, the flesh, and the devil, when we repent, we do an about-face and begin to follow our Lord Jesus Christ.

CHALLENGE QUESTIONS:

- How does Saul's experience on the Damascus Road illustrate repentance (Acts 9:1-18)?

- Have you ever said "I'm sorry" after you've been caught but didn't mean it?

- Did you keep on doing the thing that got you in trouble?

- How is that different from biblical repentance?

PRAYER:

Our Father, we "humble ourselves, pray, and seek your face. Will you hear from heaven, and forgive our sins" (2 Chronicles 7:14)? Cleanse us through the blood of Christ and send your Holy Spirit so that we can "walk in newness of life" (Rom. 6:4), in obedience to your Word. In Jesus' name we pray, Amen.

SHORTER CATECHISM
QUESTION 88

Q88 | **WHAT ARE THE OUTWARD AND ORDINARY MEANS WHEREBY CHRIST COMMUNICATETH TO US THE BENEFITS OF REDEMPTION?**

A.   The outward and ordinary means whereby Christ communicateth to us the benefits of redemption are, his ordinances, especially the Word, sacraments, and prayer, all which are made effectual to the elect for salvation.

EXPLANATION:

You and I live in a day when it's easy to communicate with one another – even with people from all over the world. Think of the power of our little hand-held devices: we can email, text, video conference, and, if we're forced to – even make a phone call! Of course, there's nothing better than live communication: hearing one another's voices, seeing one another's reactions, and speaking clearly so there's no confusion.

Did you know that our Lord Jesus Christ communicates to us live and in person? He does so through His "outward and ordinary means." Those are: the Word, sacraments, and prayer. You may notice by looking at your church bulletin that these are the central activities of worship. Why? Because Jesus promises to be present when we hear His Word (Revelation 1:12-13, 20), when we pray (Psalm 22:22, Hebrews 2:12), and when we observe the sacraments (Matthew 28:19-20; Luke 22:19-20). It's also the pattern our Lord has given us in Scripture. Consider how the early church worshiped:

> "So those who received his word were baptized, and there were added that day about three thousand souls. And they devoted themselves to the apostles' teaching and the fellowship, to the breaking of bread and the prayers" (Acts 2:41-42).

The Apostles' teaching is "code" for the preaching and hearing of God's Word. The breaking of bread is "code" for the Lord's Supper, one of the sacraments, along with baptism. And the prayers here would be all types, "supplications, prayers, intercessions, and thanksgivings" (1 Tim. 2:1), including the singing of "psalms, and hymns, and spiritual songs" (Ephesians 5:19; Colossians 3:16).

So exactly what happens when we meet with Jesus in the Word, sacraments, and prayer? The catechism says that He effectively, powerfully pours out "the benefits of redemption," the blessings of His salvation upon His people. Like those early converts we read about in Acts 2, the Lord saved them when they heard His Word preached because, "faith comes from hearing, and hearing through the word of Christ" (Romans 10:17). We're also "built up in the most holy faith when we pray in the Holy Spirit, keeping ourselves in the love of God" (Jude 20-21). And we're reminded of God's covenant promises when we see His love for us displayed in the waters of baptism and in the bread and cup of communion. Yes! Jesus uses all of these to grow us in "faith, hope, and love" (1 Corinthians 13:13).

Luke beautifully describes Christ's powerful, effective work in the early church through the means of grace:

> "Awe came upon every soul...And all who believed were together and had all things in common...distributing... to all, as any had need. And day by day, attending the temple together and breaking bread in their homes, they received their food with glad and generous hearts, praising God and having favor with all the people. And the Lord added to their number day by day those who were being saved" (Acts 2:43-47).

Aren't you glad that Jesus still speaks to us and blesses us through His means of grace?

CHALLENGE QUESTIONS:

- What's your favorite way to communicate with a friend?
- How does Jesus communicate with us?
- What happens to us when He speaks through His Word, sacrament, and prayer?

PRAYER:

Heavenly Father, through your means of grace, "build us up until we all attain the unity of the faith and the knowledge of your Son, to mature manhood, to the measure of the stature of the fullness of Christ" (Ephesians 4:12-13). *In His name we pray, Amen.*

SHORTER CATECHISM
QUESTION 89

Q89 | HOW IS THE WORD MADE EFFECTUAL TO SALVATION?

A. The Spirit of God maketh the reading, but especially the preaching, of the Word, an effectual means of convincing and converting sinners, and of building them up in holiness and comfort, through faith, unto salvation.

EXPLANATION:

Don't you love the book of Acts? It's the story of how the gospel, the good news, spreads from "Jerusalem, to Judea, to Samaria, and to the end of the earth" (Acts 1:8). This happened because Jesus called the apostles to be His witnesses. He called them to preach His Word. But something, or rather Someone, had to work to make His Word effectual or effective: the Holy Spirit! Yes. As we saw in Question 31 (Effectual Calling), when the Word is preached, the Holy Spirit works in the hearts of the elect to bring them to salvation. On the day of Pentecost, more than 3,000 people came to know Jesus as Savior! The Holy Spirit's work through Peter's sermon convinced these people of their sins and converted them by faith and repentance:

> "Now when they heard this they were cut to the heart, and said to Peter and the rest of the apostles, "Brothers, what shall we do?" And Peter said to them, 'Repent and be baptized every one of you in the name of Jesus Christ for the forgiveness of your sins,'"(Acts 2:37-38).

Later on in Acts, we read that the Spirit tells Phillip to "go over and join the chariot" of an Ethiopian who was reading a passage from the Bible he couldn't understand. So, beginning with this Scripture (Isaiah 53), Philip tells him "the good news about Jesus" (Acts 8:34-35). He, too, believes and is baptized. We see the same thing in Acts 16. One Sabbath Day, Paul preaches to a group of ladies by the riverside in Philippi, including one named Lydia. That very morning, "the Lord opened her heart to pay attention to what was said by Paul" (Acts 16:13-14). She, too, responds to the Spirit's work by trusting in Christ.

Now, the Spirit's working through God's Word doesn't stop at our conversion. The Spirit continues to give life (John 6:63). He changes us "from one degree of glory to another" as we behold the face of Jesus in His Word (2 Corinthians 3:18). Not only are we made "wise for salvation through faith in Christ Jesus," we are "built up and given the inheritance among all those who are sanctified" (Acts 20:32). Through the power of the Spirit, all Scripture is "profitable for teaching, for reproof, for correction, and for training in righteousness, that the man of God may be complete, equipped for every good work" (I1 Timothy 3:16-17).

It is true, as the catechism reminds us, that the preaching of God's Word in gathered worship is the primary way the Spirit convinces, converts, comforts, and makes us holy" (Romans 10:15-17). But He also works when we read the Scriptures on our own, with our families, in Bible studies, and in Sunday School. When we read and meditate on God's Word, not only do we "bear fruit" (Psalm 1:3) we come to Jesus, who alone has "the words of eternal life" (John 6:68).

CHALLENGE QUESTIONS:

- How did the Holy Spirit work in the book of Acts to convince and convert people?

- Read Psalm 119:97-104. Name some of the ways that God's Word builds us up when we read it.

PRAYER:

Heavenly Father, may your words be sweet to our taste, sweeter than honey to our mouths. As your Spirit works through your Word, give us understanding so that we hate every false way and love your righteousness (Psalm 119:97-104). In Jesus' name we pray, Amen.

SHORTER CATECHISM
QUESTION 90

Q90 | HOW IS THE WORD TO BE READ AND HEARD, THAT IT MAY BECOME EFFECTUAL TO SALVATION?

A. That the Word may become effectual to salvation, we must attend thereunto with diligence, preparation, and prayer; receive it with faith and love, lay it up in our hearts, and practice it in our lives.

EXPLANATION:

There's nothing quite like sitting down to a beautiful and tasty meal, like a perfectly grilled steak, baked potato, and a nice green salad! But we know that kind of meal doesn't just magically appear on our plates! It takes diligence, paying close attention while shopping for the best ingredients, and also to make sure that the food is cooked to the right temperature. Additionally, it takes preparation, from washing potatoes, to cutting vegetables, to firing up the grill, to rubbing the steak with spices. All of this and more goes into the enjoyment of a delicious steak supper. Have you ever thought that if we're to feast upon the Word of God, that we're also to prepare? That's what Question 90 is all about!

As we come to God's Word, whether to read it on our own, or to hear it preached in worship, we are to prepare. Maybe your church publishes the bulletin ahead of worship. If so, the night before, read through the various passages for the day so that you're even more prepared to hear the Scriptures read and preached. When preparing to read the Bible on our own, we might want to set a certain time and place each day that is quiet and avoids distractions.

Of course, the best preparation is prayer. We can ask the Holy Spirit to speak through the Word He inspired. We can pray with the Psalmist: "Open my eyes, that I may behold wondrous things out of your law" (Psalm 119:18). Because our sins cloud the clear teaching of Scripture, it's also good to pray that we will "put away all malice and all deceit and hypocrisy and envy and all slander. Like newborn infants, (may we) long for the pure spiritual milk (of the Word) so that by it we may grow up into salvation" (1 Peter 2:1-2).

Let's also pray for the Spirit's help in receiving God's Word in faith, removing doubt and strengthening our trust in the truth of Scripture. And as we hear of God's love for us in His works of creation, providence, and redemption, let's also pray that the Spirit would increase our love for Him and for one another.

But if God's Word is to be most effective, we also need to memorize it. "so that we might not sin against Him" (Ps. 119:11) and so that we have the "sword of the Spirit" always at the ready (Eph. 6:17). When we memorize Scripture, this means that we will always be able to "delight in God's Word as we meditate on it day and night" (Ps. 1:2). It's not enough just to hear or read the Word. That would be like preparing a delicious meal and merely staring at it instead of digging in! No, as James commands us:

"... be doers of the word, and not hearers only... For if anyone is a hearer of the word and not a doer, he is like a man who looks intently at his natural face in a mirror. For he looks at himself and goes away and at once forgets what he was like" (James 1:22-24).

CHALLENGE QUESTIONS:

- How should we prepare to read and hear God's Word?

- What are some ways that help you pay attention during sermons or Bible devotions?

- When is the best time for you to read the Bible so that there are fewer distractions?

- The best place?

PRAYER:

Heavenly Father, may our reading and hearing of your Word be "mixed with faith" (Hebrews 4:2). May your Holy Spirit use it to stir up our love for you and one another. May we hear the voice of our Good Shepherd and then follow Him in obedience. In Jesus' name we pray, Amen.

SHORTER CATECHISM
QUESTIONS 91-93

Q91 | HOW DO THE SACRAMENTS BECOME EFFECTUAL MEANS OF SALVATION?

A.   The sacraments become effectual means of salvation, not from any virtue in them, or in him that doth administer them, but only by the blessing of Christ, and the working of His Spirit in them that by faith receive them.

Q92 | WHAT IS A SACRAMENT?

A.   A sacrament is a holy ordinance instituted by Christ, wherein, by sensible signs, Christ, and the benefits of the new covenant, are represented, sealed, and applied to believers.

Q93 | WHICH ARE THE SACRAMENTS OF THE NEW TESTAMENT?

A. The sacraments of the New Testament are, baptism, and the Lord's Supper.

EXPLANATION:

Have you ever had a teacher who used visual aids to help you understand a school lesson? Maybe a model of an atom, a history timeline, a graph or chart that showed information in visible form? It's not that the information is different; it's just sometimes clearer when we can see it. In the same way, the sacraments help us to see what the Bible teaches us about the work of our Savior Jesus Christ. Our Heavenly Father knows that we need visual reminders of His love, and He has given them to us in the sacraments.

Augustine, the great theologian of the early church, is attributed with this simple definition of a sacrament: "a sacrament is an outward sign of an inward grace."[21] The sacraments show us something about the blessings we receive because we are God's covenant children. As we read in Question 93, baptism and the Lord's Supper are the two sacraments Jesus instituted or established for us to keep until He comes again (Matthew 28:19, 1 Corinthians 11:23-26). We'll talk more about them in the devotions to come, but these two sacraments are signs, visual pictures of God's grace to us in Jesus Christ.

---

21 Augustine, *On Catechizing the Uninstructed* in *The Works of St. Augustine,* Vol. 3, 50.26, in Philip Schaff, ed., *Nicene and Post-Nicene Fathers,* (Grand Rapids: Eerdmans, 1956), p. 312.

It's important to remember, though, that the minister doesn't magically make these sacraments effective. Though only ordained pastors should baptize and lead the Lord's Supper, it is Jesus Himself, through His Holy Spirit, who works in the hearts of believers to bless them. As Paul writes:

"So neither he who plants nor he who waters is anything, but only God who gives the growth" (1 Corinthians 3:7).

Keep in mind that not all who participate in the sacraments receive God's blessing. It's only those who receive them by faith, who trust in Jesus Christ alone for their salvation. You see, the sacraments are seals of God's promise, like the signet ring of a king pressed into wax to let you know that his letter is authentic. Through the sacraments, our Heavenly Father pledges to us that "all the promises of God find their Yes in Jesus Christ. That is why it is through him that we utter our Amen to God for his glory" (2 Corinthians 1:20). If we take the sacraments without faith, they have no good effect on us. Just the opposite! (1 Corinthians 11:29). But if we believe in Jesus, when we participate in baptism and the Lord's Supper, He confirms what we read in Scripture and strengthens us in faith, hope, and love.

CHALLENGE QUESTIONS:

- Can you think of a time when a visual aid (diagram, picture, map, YouTube video) helped you learn something?

- Name the two sacraments.

- How are the sacraments signs?

- How do they act as seals?

PRAYER:

Heavenly Father, may we "taste and see that you are good" (Psalm 34:8) as we partake of the sacraments. Give us the eyes of faith so that we see Christ in the waters of baptism and as we eat the bread and drink the cup of communion. These things we ask in Jesus' name, Amen.

SHORTER CATECHISM
QUESTIONS 94 & 95

Q94 | WHAT IS BAPTISM?

A. Baptism is a sacrament, wherein the washing with water in the name of the Father, and of the Son, and of the Holy Ghost (Spirit), doth signify and seal our ingrafting into Christ, and partaking of the benefits of the covenant of grace, and our engagement to be the Lord's.

Q95 | TO WHOM IS BAPTISM TO BE ADMINISTERED?

A. Baptism is not to be administered to any that are out of the visible church, till they profess their faith in Christ, and obedience to Him; but the infants of such as are members of the visible church are to be baptized.

EXPLANATION:

Somewhere in your home, you may have pictures of the day you were baptized as an infant or young child. Your father or mother may be holding you in front of the church while the pastor is pouring or sprinkling water on your head. There may be other photographs of you with grandparents, aunts and uncles, and other family members to celebrate God's special promise that "He will be a God to us and to our children after us" (Genesis 17:7, Acts 2:39). Others of you may have been baptized when you were older, when you professed faith in Jesus Christ as your Savior and Lord. In our last devotion, we learned that the sacraments act as pictures (signs) and promises (seals) of God's mercy to us in Christ. What does baptism picture and promise?

First, the water of baptism pictures the washing away of our sins through the blood of Jesus Christ. As Ananias says to Saul after his Damascus Road experience: "Rise and be baptized and wash away your sins, calling on his name" (Acts 22:16). Just like we use water to wash away dirt from our bodies, the pouring or sprinkling of baptism symbolizes that our "hearts have been sprinkled clean from an evil conscience and our bodies washed with pure water" (Hebrews 10:22).

In addition, baptism pictures our new life in Christ through "the washing of regeneration and renewal of the Holy Spirit, whom he poured out on us richly through Jesus Christ our Savior" (Titus 3:5-6). We now belong to God as we are baptized "in the name of the Father, and of the Son, and of the Holy Spirit" (Matthew 28:19). We're "ingrafted into Christ." Like a gardener who can take a wild branch from one type of tree and graft or join it to another type of tree to create something new, so our

Heavenly Father joins us to Jesus Christ, the True and Living Vine, so that we now live, grow, and bear fruit (John 15:1-5).

Because we are now "new creations in Christ" (2 Corinthians 5:17), we enjoy "every spiritual blessing in the heavenly places" (Ephesians 1:3). Our baptism is a picture of our union (unbreakable bond) with Christ. We are now "engaged to be the Lord's." Sin no longer has authority or dominion over us (Romans 6:14). Instead, "we were buried...with him by baptism into death, in order that, just as Christ was raised from the dead by the glory of the Father, we too might walk in newness of life" (Romans 6:4).

That's right! God not only pictures, but also promises our cleansing from sin and our new life in the sacrament of baptism. But these blessings aren't given automatically through the pouring or sprinkling of water on the head of an infant or an adult. These promises picture the saving work of our Lord Jesus Christ and must be received by faith, by trusting in Jesus Christ alone for our salvation.

CHALLENGE QUESTIONS:

- Can you describe a baptism service at your church?
- What two things does baptism picture and promise?
- Who should be baptized?

PRAYER:

Heavenly Father, thank you for the pictures and promises of baptism. Thank you for "forgiving our sins and cleansing us from all unrighteousness" (1 John 1:9). Thank you for "causing us to be born again to a living hope through the resurrection of Jesus Christ from the dead" (1 Peter 1:3). In Jesus' name we pray, Amen.

SHORTER CATECHISM
QUESTION 96

Q96 | WHAT IS THE LORD'S SUPPER?

A. The Lord's Supper is a sacrament, wherein, by giving and receiving bread and wine, according to Christ's appointment, his death is showed forth, and the worthy receivers are, not after a corporal and carnal manner, but by faith, made partakers of his body and blood, with all his benefits, to their spiritual nourishment, and growth in grace.

EXPLANATION:

Do you have a favorite family meal? Maybe it's Thanksgiving with turkey, dressing, sweet potatoes, a cornucopia of vegetables, topped off by homemade pumpkin pie. Maybe it's a birthday dinner your mother makes with a special cake for dessert. Or something from a favorite restaurant you enjoy on important occasions. Did you know that the Lord's Supper is God's special meal with His family? Jesus Christ Himself meets with us and we feed on Him by faith.

You may remember in Exodus that God Himself meets with Moses and the seventy elders of Israel on Mt. Sinai, where He appears to them. We're told that "under His feet as it were a pavement of sapphire stone...they beheld (looked at) God, and ate and drank" (Exodus 24:10-11). Wow! Can you imagine what it would have been like to eat and drink with God that day? You and I get that same opportunity every time we gather for the Lord's Supper. Jesus Christ is present with us! No. We don't see Him with our eyes, but He's with us through His Holy Spirit. And He does some amazing things when we eat and drink with Him!

First, Jesus reminds us of His death through the bread and the cup. This is how He introduces the Lord's Supper in the Upper Room, just hours before He would suffer and die on the cross:

> "Now as they were eating, Jesus took bread, and after blessing it broke it and gave it to the disciples, and said, 'Take, eat; this is my body.' And he took a cup, and when he had given thanks he gave it to them, saying, 'Drink of it, all of you, for this is my blood of the covenant, which is poured out for many for the forgiveness of sins'" (Matthew 26:26-28).

When we eat the bread, we're reminded of Christ's body sacrificed in our place. When we drink the cup, we're reminded of His blood spilled so that we might be forgiven. And we're filled with thanks for what Jesus has done to save us from our sins!

But Jesus does more than remind us of what He's done for us in the past. He also feeds us in the present. Just like bread satisfies our hunger and wine relieves our thirst, when we participate in the Lord's Supper, the Holy Spirit feeds our faith and grows us more into the image of Christ:

"The cup of blessing that we bless, is it not a participation in the blood of Christ? The bread that we break, is it not a participation in the body of Christ? Because there is one bread, we who are many are one body, for we all partake of the one bread" (1 Corinthians 10:16-17).

Finally, when we eat and drink the Lord's Supper, trusting in Jesus Christ, our Heavenly Father refreshes us with His love. He seals His promise that we are His royal children, heirs to all the treasures of His kingdom (Romans 8:14-17). When we sit down with our brothers and sisters in Christ, we're reminded that we have a seat at His table, both in this life and in our Father's house forevermore (Psalm 23:5-6)!

CHALLENGE QUESTIONS:

- What is your favorite family meal?
- What does the bread represent in the Lord's Supper?
- What does the cup represent?
- Name some promises that God reminds us of at communion.

PRAYER:

Heavenly Father, we thank you for the blessings of the Lord's Supper! Thank you that Jesus meets with us and feeds us when we come to your table. May we "taste and see that He is good" (Psalm 34:8). In Jesus' name we pray, Amen.

SHORTER CATECHISM
QUESTION 97

Q97 | WHAT IS REQUIRED FOR THE WORTHY RECEIVING OF THE LORD'S SUPPER?

A.   It is required of them that would worthily partake of the Lord's Supper, that they examine themselves of their knowledge to discern the Lord's body, of their faith to feed upon Him, of their repentance, love, and new obedience; lest, coming unworthily, they eat and drink judgment to themselves.

EXPLANATION:

Imagine you're hosting someone very important for dinner, like a king, queen, president, or senator. What would you do to prepare for the evening? Give the house a thorough cleaning? Spread a new tablecloth and set the table with the finest china? Select the best food and drink to serve? I'm sure we would do all these things and more to honor our esteemed guest! Since we're meeting with "the Holy One," (John 6:69), "the King of kings and Lord of lords" (Revelation 19:16) when we come to the communion table, we, too must prepare. We must prepare our hearts by examining them.

Just like we examine slides under a microscope, Paul says we're carefully to "examine ourselves" (1 Corinthians 11:28-29) before we come to the Lord's Supper. The first thing we're to examine is our "knowledge to discern the Lord's body." This means that we must understand what's going on in the Lord's Supper, that the bread represents Christ's body and that the cup represents His blood. We must understand that communion pictures His one-time sacrifice for the sins of His people.

But it's not enough just to know what communion means. We also must have faith. We must truly trust that Jesus lived, died, and rose again for us. If we take the Lord's Supper in faith, then Jesus feeds us. As He tells His disciples, "For my flesh is true food, and my blood is true drink" (John 6:55). Yet, Paul warns that even true believers can come in a way that displeases God and brings us under His discipline:

> "Whoever, therefore, eats the bread or drinks the cup of the Lord in an unworthy manner will be guilty concerning the body and blood of the Lord" (1 Corinthians 11:27).

To avoid His displeasure, judgment, and discipline, we must look at our hearts to see if we are truly repentant, which means being sorry for sin and turning away from it in new obedience. Since communion is the time that we celebrate God's love for us and our love for one another, we need to examine our love for Him, for our neighbor, and for the lost. What a wonderful opportunity the Lord gives us before the Lord's Supper to get right with Him and with our brothers and sisters in Christ. This is a great time for us to "draw near to God" in prayer, knowing that He will "draw near to us," as we "cleanse our hands and purify our hearts" (James 4:8), seeking His forgiveness through the blood of Jesus Christ.

Keep in mind that none of us, on our own, are worthy to receive the Lord's Supper. It's only by God's grace that we believe in Christ (Ephesians 2:8-9). Our repentance, love, and new obedience all spring forth from the Holy Spirit's work in our lives (Titus 3:3-8; Galatians 5:22-23). And even in those times when our walk with Jesus is weak, He calls us to feed upon Him again, saying:

> "I am the bread of life; whoever comes to me shall not hunger, and whoever believes in me shall never thirst" (John 6:35).

CHALLENGE QUESTIONS:

- What would be your favorite meal to serve an important guest?
- What is one thing you can do to prepare your heart for the Lord's Supper?

PRAYER:

Heavenly Father, thank you for giving us the Lord's Supper as a time to renew our relationship with you. Every time the Lord's Supper is offered, may we prepare by examining our hearts, drawing near to you in prayer, and looking again to Jesus, "the founder and perfecter of our faith" (Hebrews 12:2). In Jesus' name we pray, Amen.

98-99

SHORTER CATECHISM
QUESTIONS 98 & 99

Q98 | WHAT IS PRAYER?

A. Prayer is an offering up of our desires unto God, for things agreeable to His will, in the name of Christ, with confession of our sins, and thankful acknowledgment of His mercies.

EXPLANATION:

Have you ever watched the joy on a baseball player's face as he rounds third base and heads for home? Well, we're heading for home in our study of the Shorter Catechism. Since Question 85, we've been talking about the "means of grace," the ways that Jesus Christ communicates with us. So far, we've seen that He speaks to us through His Word and that we see Him through the eyes of faith in the sacraments of baptism and the Lord's Supper. Now, we read that He hears us when we pray. So, the home stretch of the catechism teaches us how to pray.

Question 98 gives us a beautiful definition for prayer. Isn't it wonderful and encouraging that our Heavenly Father's ear is open to hear the desires of our hearts?

"O LORD, you hear the desire of the afflicted; You will strengthen their heart; You will incline your ear" (Psalm 10:17).

That's right! God wants us to speak to Him all the time, to "pray without ceasing...at all times in the Spirit" (1 Thessalonians 5:17, Ephesians 6:18). Jesus, our Lord, encourages us to pray with perseverance.

"Ask, and it will be given to you; seek, and you will find; knock, and it will be opened to you. For everyone who asks receives, and the one who seeks finds, and to the one who knocks it will be opened" (Matthew 7:7-8).

Of course, we're not to ask for things that are sinful or selfish. As James warns us, "You ask and do not receive, because you ask wrongly, to spend it on your passions" (James 4:3). Instead, we're to ask for things that are "agreeable to His will." This means that we are to pray for things that agree with God's Word, His revealed will. That's why Question 99 urges us to pray with Bible open:

Q99 | WHAT RULE HATH GOD GIVEN FOR OUR DIRECTION IN PRAYER?

A. **The whole Word of God is of use to direct us in prayer; but the special rule of direction is that form of prayer which Christ taught His disciples, commonly called the Lord's Prayer.**

EXPLANATION:

Over the next few devotions, we'll take a long look at the Lord's Prayer as Jesus gives us direction for praising God, confessing our sins, asking for His help, and thanking our Heavenly Father for His blessings.

Not only are we to pray according to Scripture, we are also to pray in the name of Jesus Christ. You see, He is our Great High Priest (see Question 25), the one who prays for us at the Father's right hand (1 John 2:1, Hebrews 8:1). Because of His death for us, He is the "one mediator between God and men" (1 Timothy 2:5). Through Jesus, we gain access to the throne of grace and have confidence that we will "receive mercy and find grace to help in our time of need" (Hebrews 4:16).

So as we pray each day according to Scripture and in the name of Jesus, may we be encouraged by His promise: "Truly, truly, I say to you, whatever you ask of the Father in my name, he will give it to you...Ask, and you will receive, that your joy may be full" (John 16:23-24).

CHALLENGE QUESTIONS:

- Can you recite the Lord's Prayer (Mat. 6:9-13)?
- Can you name some other Scriptures that help us to pray (Book of Psalms, Philippians 4:4-7, 1 Thessalonians 5:16-18, Daniel 9:3-19)?
- Why must we pray in the name of Jesus?

PRAYER:

Heavenly Father, may we come to you in prayer with "rejoicing, not being anxious about anything, but in everything – with prayer, supplication, and thanksgiving – let us make our requests known to you" (Philippians 4:4-6). In Jesus' name we pray, Amen.

SHORTER CATECHISM
QUESTION 100

Q100 | WHAT DOTH THE PREFACE OF THE LORD'S PRAYER TEACH US?

A.   The preface of the Lord's Prayer, which is, *Our Father which art in heaven*, teacheth us to draw near to God with all holy reverence and confidence, as children to a father, able and ready to help us; and that we should pray with and for others.

EXPLANATION:

Most of the books we read include a preface. A preface is an introduction that lets us know what to expect from the author. It also acts as an invitation into the author's mind as we turn the pages and discover his or her thoughts. The preface of the Lord's Prayer invites us into a close relationship with our Heavenly Father.

That's right! When we pray, "Our Father," we're speaking to the one who loves us so much that He has our names engraved on the palms of His hands (Isaiah 49:16), keeps count of our tossings and tears (Psalm 56:8), and even numbers the hairs on our heads (Luke 12:7). He's the One who lovingly chose us in Christ to be His adopted children, even before the world began (Ephesians 1:4-6)! And because He is the Holy one "who made heaven and earth" (Psalm 115:15), we honor Him by speaking to Him with reverence and awe (Hebrews 12:28). At the same time, we come with confidence, joy, and assurance because our Heavenly Father delights to hear the prayers of His children:

> "For you did not receive the spirit of slavery to fall back into fear, but you have received the Spirit of adoption as sons, by whom we cry, "Abba! Father!" The Spirit himself bears witness with our spirit that we are children of God, and if children, then heirs—heirs of God and fellow heirs with Christ" (Rom. 8:15-17).

When we ask for things according to the Father's will in the name of His Son Jesus, we know that He will withhold "no good thing" from us (Ps. 84:11). As Jesus tells us, if sinful, earthly parents "know how to give good things to [their] children, how much more will [our] Father who is in heaven give good things to those who ask Him!" (Matt. 7:9-11).

Keep in mind, too, that Jesus doesn't teach us to pray, "My Father," but "Our Father." His invitation isn't only to pray for ourselves, but to pray "with and for others." This includes the prayers Christians offer together during times of worship, at weekly prayer meetings, in small group Bible Studies, with our families at home, or with a friend before a meal. You see, it's a real privilege to pray for our loved ones, for our church family, for missionaries, for our leaders, and for all of those who are in need. As Paul encourages Timothy:

"I urge that supplications, prayers, intercessions, and thanksgivings be made for all people" (1 Tim. 2:1).

What an invitation is offered to us in the preface of the Lord's Prayer! Our Heavenly Father calls His children to draw near to Him individually and together as the body of Christ. How should we answer His invitation? We should "be constant in prayer" (Romans 12:12), knowing that our Heavenly Father is "able to do far more abundantly than all that we ask or think" (Ephesians 3:20) for His beloved children!

CHALLENGE QUESTIONS:

- What is a preface?
- Do you read or skip them in books?
- Why shouldn't we skip the preface to the Lord's Prayer?

PRAYER:

Our Father, hear from heaven our voices as we draw near to you in prayer. May we pray with confidence because "Your arm isn't too short to save, and your ear isn't too dull to hear" (Isaiah 59:1). In Jesus' name we pray, Amen.

SHORTER CATECHISM
QUESTION 101

Q101 | WHAT DO WE PRAY FOR IN THE FIRST PETITION?

A. In the first petition, which is *Hallowed be thy name*, we pray that God would enable us, and others, to glorify Him in all that whereby He maketh Himself known; and that He would dispose all things to His own glory.

EXPLANATION:

When you hear the word petition, what comes to mind? You might think of a letter signed by people to get a president, governor, school principal or some other leader to investigate a problem or to change a harmful policy. Maybe you've petitioned your parents for a bigger allowance! Sadly, most petitions are ignored. Not so when we petition or ask things from our Heavenly Father! The Shorter Catechism divides the Lord's Prayer into six petitions or requests. The first three focus on God, while the final three focus on us.

The first petition is: "Hallowed be thy name." We don't often use the word "hallowed" anymore, but it means to make something holy, to set it apart, to give it special status. So hallowing God's name is the opposite of taking His name in vain, taking it lightly. When we pray, "Hallowed be thy name," we're asking that God's name would be glorified or magnified above everyone and everything else. This is how the angels address our Triune God: "Holy, holy, holy is the LORD of hosts; the whole earth is full of his glory!" (Isaiah 6:3).

In this first petition, we're asking that God would make Himself known throughout the world in His works of creation, providence, and redemption. We might pray the following:

- That our Heavenly Father would be glorified as our Creator as we enjoy a beautiful spring day through its bright blue sky, budding flowers, and green grass.

- That He would be glorified as "The LORD (who) will provide" (Genesis 22:14) as He supplies us with food, shelter, and clothing.

- That our "Lord and Savior Jesus Christ" (2 Peter 1:11) would be glorified as He "purifies a people for Himself as His own possession" (Titus 2:14) through His "Spirit of holiness" (Romans 1:4).

- That the love of Jesus would be glorified in the way that we love one another, so that all people will know we're His disciples (John 13:35).

- That "the Light of the World" (John 8:12) would shine in us, so that the lost "might see our good works and give glory to our Father in heaven" (Matthew 5:16).

When we pray, "Hallowed be thy name," we're also asking that God would "work out everything for His own glory,"[22] that whatever happens – whether good or bad, big or small – would serve His purpose of making His name great.

Do you see why Jesus wants us to start our prayers focusing on God and not on ourselves? When we start with our personal concerns, we're much more likely to ask for things that bring glory to ourselves rather than to our Triune God.

CHALLENGE QUESTIONS:

- What would you like to petition (or request) of a political leader?
- Can you think of some names for the Triune God?
- How can you turn those names into praises?
- Why should we start our prayers thinking about God rather than ourselves?

PRAYER:

Triune God, may we "ascribe to you the glory and strength due to your Holy name" (Psalm 29:1-2). May you be glorified in everything that we say, think, feel, and do today. And may everything that happens in heaven and on the earth magnify you. In Jesus' name we pray, Amen.

---

22 Douglas Kelly and Philip Rollinson, *The Shorter Catechism in Modern English* (Presbyterian and Reformed Publishing Company, Phillipsburg, NJ) 1986, p. 22.

102

SHORTER CATECHISM
QUESTION 102

Q102 | WHAT DO WE PRAY FOR IN THE SECOND PETITION?

A. In the second petition, which is, *Thy Kingdom Come*, we pray that Satan's kingdom may be destroyed; and that the kingdom of grace may be advanced, ourselves and others brought into it, and kept in it; and that the kingdom of glory may be hastened.

EXPLANATION:

Have you ever thought of yourself as part of a kingdom? Kings, queens, knights and castles seem like fantasies to ordinary people, particularly if you live in the United States, but we are all subjects in the greatest kingdom of all: "The kingdom of our Lord and of His Christ" (Revelation 11:15)! And the second petition of the Lord's Prayer invites us to pray for the success of our King Jesus in advancing His Kingdom.

Just like we learn in our history books and on today's world stage, kingdoms have enemies and often go to war with one another. The Bible tells us that from Adam's fall, the kingdom of Satan has been at war with the kingdom of Christ. Thankfully, we know that Jesus has already won the war because He has given Satan the death blow. He has "bruised the serpent's head" (Genesis 3:15) through His life, death, and resurrection. Even now, King Jesus is seated at His Father's right hand, putting His enemies under His feet (Psalm 110:1). But even though Satan is a defeated enemy, he's still very dangerous and much stronger than we are on our own. And in his remaining time, he lives to make war on Christ and His church (Revelation 12:7-17). That's why we must pray for Satan's kingdom to be fully and finally destroyed:

> "For we do not wrestle against flesh and blood, but against the rulers, against the authorities, against the cosmic powers over this present darkness, against the spiritual forces of evil in the heavenly places" (Ephesians 6:12).

That's right! We don't fight with worldly weapons like swords, guns, tanks, missiles, or fighter jets. Instead, our Lord Jesus clothes us with spiritual armor (Ephesians 6:13-17). Above all, He urges us to pray:

> "...at all times in the Spirit, with all prayer and supplication. To that end, keep alert with all perseverance, making supplication for all the saints." (Ephesians 6:18).

At the top of our prayer list should be "the advance of the kingdom of grace." We should pray for our local church – that the gospel would be preached, that God's people would grow to be more like Christ, and that the lost would respond in faith and in repentance. We should pray that God's people would tell their neighbors about Jesus. We should pray for those who are planting new churches, those serving in campus ministries, and those who are called to world missions. There's no greater privilege than to pray that the Holy Spirit would draw people to saving faith "from every nation, from all tribes and peoples and languages" (Revelation 7:9).

Remembering Jesus' promise, "Surely I am coming soon" (Revelation 22:20), fills us with hope. How else ought we to respond but by praying, "Amen. Come, Lord Jesus." May the kingdom of glory come so that the full number of your people may stand "before the throne and before the Lamb, clothed in white robes, with palm branches in their hands, crying out with a loud voice, 'Salvation belongs to our God who sits on the throne and to the Lamb!'" (Revelation 7:9-10). Then and only then will His kingdom fully come.

CHALLENGE QUESTIONS:

- If Satan has already been defeated, why do we still need to pray that his kingdom will be destroyed?

- Name some missionaries that your church or family supports. How can you pray for them?

- What else can you do to encourage them in their kingdom work?

PRAYER:

King of kings and Lord of lords, we pray that your kingdom would come here on the earth as you save and sanctify sinners. We pray for pastors, missionaries, and all Christians as we seek to make disciples of all nations. May you come quickly, O Lord, so that you, "the God of peace will finally crush Satan under your feet" (Romans 16:20). In Jesus' name, Amen.

SHORTER CATECHISM
QUESTION 103

Q103 | WHAT DO WE PRAY FOR IN THE THIRD PETITION?

A.   In the third petition which is, *Thy will be done in earth as it is in heaven*, we pray, that God by His grace, would make us able and willing to know, obey, and submit to His will in all things, as the angels do in heaven.

EXPLANATION:

When we looked at Question 7, we learned about the decrees of God, "His eternal purpose, according to the counsel of His will, whereby, for His own glory, He hath foreordained whatsoever comes to pass." This is one aspect of God's will, that He has decreed or foreordained everything that happens throughout the universe for all time. We should certainly pray that His perfect plan would unfold in our lives and throughout the world because we know that it is for our good (Romans 8:28) and for His glory. We also need to pray that we'll submit, that we'll accept His will, even when times are tough. At the same time, this question also deals with God's revealed will, His holy Word.

When we pray *"Thy will be done in earth as it is in heaven,"* we're asking for God's help to know and understand the Bible when we read it and hear it taught. But we're praying for even more. We're praying that the Holy Spirit would make us willing to obey God's Word and to come under its authority for our lives – in all things! We're praying like our Lord Jesus in the Garden of Gethsemane the night before He would suffer and die, "Not as I will, but as you will" (Matthew 26:39). We're praying that we'll obey God's voice just "like the angels do in heaven" (Psalm 103:20-21).

I don't know about you, but sometimes I have a hard time obeying and submitting to God's Word. Because of our sin and selfishness, we want to do things that please ourselves instead of serving the Lord and our neighbors. When we feel like we don't want to obey, we need to pray like the Psalmist: "Teach me to do your will, for you are my God! Let your good Spirit lead me on level ground" (Psalm 143:10). And take heart! Our Lord will answer this prayer. As He says through Ezekiel: "I will put my Spirit within you and cause you to walk in my statutes and be careful to obey my rules" (Ezekiel 36:27).

What blessing is ours when the Holy Spirit works in our hearts so that we're willing to obey God's Word! As the Lord assures Israel before they enter the Promised Land:

> "If you obey the commandments of the LORD your God that I command you today, by loving the LORD your God, by walking in his ways, and by keeping his commandments and his statutes and his rules, then you

shall live and multiply, and the LORD your God will bless you in the land that you are entering to take possession of it" (Deuteronomy 30:16).

Just remember – it's only by God's grace that we have strength to obey and enjoy His blessing. That's why we must pray, *"Thy will be done in earth as it is in heaven!"*

CHALLENGE QUESTIONS:

- When do you find it hard to obey your parents?

- When do you find it hard to obey God's Word?

- How does Jesus' prayer in the Garden of Gethsemane encourage us when we have a hard time submitting to God's will?

- What promises does God give to those who obey His Word?

PRAYER:

Heavenly Father, may we "delight to do your will" because "Your law is written on our hearts" (Psalm 40:8 NKJV). Help us to "trust and obey, for there's no other way to be happy in Jesus but to trust and obey." In Jesus' name we pray, Amen.

SHORTER CATECHISM
QUESTION 104

Q104 | WHAT DO WE PRAY FOR IN THE FOURTH PETITION?

A. In the fourth petition, which is, *Give us this day our daily bread*, we pray that of God's free gift we may receive a competent portion of the good things of this life, and enjoy His blessing with them.

EXPLANATION:

"God is great; God is good. Let us thank Him for our food. By His hands we all are fed; give us, Lord, our daily bread." I'm pretty sure that this was the first prayer I learned. Is that the same for you? Maybe your parents taught it to you, or you memorized it in Sunday School, or even in kindergarten. This prayer has truly stood the test of time and has taught generations to be thankful for the food we enjoy at each meal. To be sure, this simple prayer reflects what Jesus teaches us to pray in the fourth petition. It reminds us of God's greatness

– His strength, His wisdom, His ability – to feed us. He's the One who miraculously supplied bread from heaven (manna), water, and quail for His children in the middle of the desert land (Psalm 78:15-16, 21-29). Surely, we can trust in His power today to provide our daily bread.

And not only is our God great, He is also good. He cares not only for our souls, but also for our bodies! Not only does He supply food to all of His creation (Psalm 104:10-30), He also provides clothing (Matthew 6:25-33), shelter, the very air that we breathe, and grants us good health to enjoy His beautiful world. As the brother of our Lord wrote, "Every good and every perfect gift is from above, coming down from the Father of lights with whom there is no variation or shadow due to change" (James 1:17 NKJV). How kind, loving, gracious, and good is our God! Though we deserve nothing, He pours out His blessing upon us in just the right measure.

Notice that Jesus teaches us to pray daily. He truly wants us to live "hand-to-mouth," relying on Him for all "the good things of this life." We're not just to pray occasionally or when we're in desperate need. Instead, we're to remember that when our Father opens His hands, we are filled with good things and that when He hides His face, we are dismayed (Psalm 104:28-29). Praying daily for our physical needs keeps us dependent on our great and good Heavenly Father.

The catechism also urges us to pray to receive "a competent portion" of good things from God. This reflects the wisdom of proverbs: "Give me neither poverty nor riches; feed me with the food that is needful for me, lest I be full and deny you, and say, 'Who is the Lord?' or lest I be poor and steal and profane the name of my God (Proverbs 30:8-9). Yes! The Lord desires us to be content with His good gifts. As Paul reminds us:

"...godliness with contentment is great gain, for we brought nothing into the world, and we cannot take anything out of the world. But if we have food and clothing, with these we will be content" (1 Timothy 6:6-8).

Let us thank our Heavenly Father for all His good and perfect gifts!

CHALLENGE QUESTIONS:

- What was the first prayer that you learned and where did you learn it?
- Why does Jesus teach us to pray daily for our physical needs?
- According to Proverbs 30:8-9 what's the danger of having too much?
- What's the danger of having too little?

PRAYER:

Our great and good Heavenly Father, will you supply our needs today? Thank you that Jesus is the Bread of Life, filling us with spiritual life through the Spirit. Would you provide for our physical needs, too? Give us exactly what we need so that we're content as we continue to depend on your blessing. In Jesus' name, Amen.

SHORTER CATECHISM
QUESTION 105

Q105 | WHAT DO WE PRAY FOR IN THE FIFTH PETITION?

A. In the fifth petition which is, *And forgive us our debts as we forgive our debtors*, we pray that God, for Christ's sake, would freely pardon all our sins; which we are the rather encouraged to ask, because by His grace we are enabled from the heart to forgive others.

EXPLANATION:

Canceled! We live in a strange time, don't we? A time when the world pretends to be more tolerant and inclusive. But also a time when people are routinely canceled or cut off from society for saying or doing something inappropriate. Sometimes, you might be canceled simply for failing to go along with popular opinion. Still, others are canceled just for associating with someone seen to be on the wrong side of an issue. Thankfully, our God doesn't cancel us when we sin.

Instead, He invites us to come to Him, confessing our sins, "For He is faithful and just to forgive us our sins and to cleanse us from all unrighteousness" (1 John 1:9).

That's right! We can pray with confidence, "*forgive us our debts*," because Jesus paid the debt we owed for our sins. As Paul teaches, "For the wages of sin is death, but the free gift of God is eternal life in Christ Jesus our Lord" (Romans 6:23). But even though our debt is paid in full when we come to faith in Jesus Christ (see Shorter Catechism Question 33), you and I still sin each day in our thoughts, words, and actions. And though true Christians are in no danger of losing our salvation when we sin, our relationship with our Heavenly Father becomes strained, distant, and cold when we fail to repent. The good news is every time we return, even after committing awful sins, we experience His blessing. Consider King David's prayer of thanksgiving after he had repented from his sin of adultery and murder:

"Blessed is the one whose transgression is forgiven, whose sin is covered. Blessed is the man against whom the LORD counts no iniquity, and in whose spirit there is no deceit" (Psalm 32:1-2).

What a gracious God! "He forgives all our iniquity, He heals all our diseases...He does not deal with us according to our sins, nor repay us according to our iniquities...as far as the heavens are above the earth, so great is His steadfast love toward those who fear Him. As far as the east is from the west, so far does He remove our transgression from us" (Psalm 103:3-4, 10-12).

Because He graciously forgives us, Jesus also teaches us to graciously forgive those who sin against us. Peter asks Jesus a tough question: "'How often will my brother sin against me and I forgive him? As many as seven times?' Jesus said to him

'I do not say to you seven times, but seventy-seven times!'" (Matthew 18:21-22). In other words, we are to forgive as many times as we're asked for forgiveness! Jesus is clear: "... if you forgive others their trespasses, your heavenly Father will also forgive you, but if you do not forgive others their trespasses, neither will your Father forgive your trespasses" (Matthew 6:14-15). Keep in mind that God's forgiveness is based on Christ's saving work alone; but if we're unwilling to forgive others, it means that we've never understood God's grace in forgiving the sin debt we could never repay.

Isn't it wonderful that instead of canceling us for breaking His holy commandments, our Father has canceled the debt we owed through the power of the cross? So instead of participating in Cancel Culture, let us freely forgive others as we have been freely forgiven through Jesus.

CHALLENGE QUESTIONS:

- Can you think of a time when it was hard to forgive someone who had sinned against you?

- Read Matthew 18:23-35. What do we forget about our own debt when we fail to forgive?

PRAYER:

Gracious Heavenly Father, "have mercy upon us, according to your steadfast love" (Psalm 51:1). Forgive us for our sins and give us grace to forgive those who've sinned against us. Thank you that "Jesus Paid it All" by dying on the cross for our sins. In His name we pray, Amen.

SHORTER CATECHISM
QUESTION 106

Q106 | WHAT DO WE PRAY FOR IN THE SIXTH PETITION?

A. In the sixth petition, which is, *And lead us not into temptation, but deliver us from evil*, we pray, that God would either keep us from being tempted to sin, or support and deliver us when we are tempted.

EXPLANATION:

In the previous petition from the Lord's Prayer, Jesus taught us to pray for the forgiveness of our sins. In this petition, we're asking that our Heavenly Father, in His kind providence, would keep us from sinning in the first place. As King David prays,

> "Keep back your servant also from presumptuous sins; let them not have dominion over me! Then I shall be blameless, and innocent of great transgression" (Psalm 19:13).

What a wonderful thing to pray at the beginning of each day because we're surrounded by potential temptations; whether inappropriate content on the internet, advertisements that entice us to buy items we can't afford, or to eat more food than we need. We're also tempted by others who wish to lead us astray or want us to join with them in their sin (Proverbs 1:10-19). Because we struggle to obey when faced with these and many other situations, we need to pray, "lead us not into temptation."

At the same time, God hasn't called us to live in a temptation-free bubble! Though we're to flee from temptation (Genesis 39:11-13), there are times when we simply can't avoid it as we go about our daily lives. Remember, He has called us to be His ambassadors as we go into the world making disciples. (Matthew 5:13-16; 28:19-20). Yet, as our Savior sends us, He also prays to His Father, "I do not ask that you take them out of the world, but that you keep them from the evil one" (John 17:15). We echo our Lord when we pray, "deliver us from evil."

Thankfully, we have God's sure promises of support and deliverance when temptation comes! Paul encourages us with these words:

> "No temptation has overtaken you that is not common to man. God is faithful, and he will not let you be tempted beyond your ability, but with the temptation he will also provide the way of escape, that you may be able to endure it" (1 Corinthians 10:13).

What a promise! Our temptations are never too strong for us if we ask for the Holy Spirit's help to endure and escape them. That's true even if they come from Satan: "Resist the devil, and he will flee from you. Draw near to God, and he will draw near to you" (James 4:7-8).

Of course, the hardest temptations come from within. As James also says, "each person is tempted when he is lured and enticed by his own desire" (James 1:14). That's why we need to pray each day, "Create in me a clean heart, O God, and renew a right spirit within me" (Psalm 51:10), so that we desire those things that please, honor, and glorify God.

CHALLENGE QUESTIONS:

- What are some advertisements you see that tempt you to covet?
- What does Jesus say about cutting off temptation at the source (Matthew 5:27-30)?
- Can you think of some situations where temptation is unavoidable?
- How should we pray beforehand?
- How can we pray during?
- And afterwards?

PRAYER:

Heavenly Father, we pray that you would keep us from temptation today. If it comes, give us the power of the Holy Spirit to resist it. "Renew our minds" (Romans 12:2) and "purify our hearts" (James 4:8) so that we desire to love and obey you instead of sin. In Jesus' name we pray, Amen.

SHORTER CATECHISM
QUESTION 107

Q107 | WHAT DOTH THE CONCLUSION OF THE LORD'S PRAYER TEACH US?

A. The conclusion of the Lord's Prayer, which is, *For thine is the kingdom, and the power, and the glory, forever. Amen*, teacheth us to take our encouragement in prayer from God only, and in our prayers to praise Him, ascribing kingdom, power, and glory to Him; and, in testimony of our desire, and assurance to be heard, we say, Amen.

EXPLANATION:

Do you sing a song called the Doxology in your weekly worship? The most famous one was written by a man named Thomas Ken all the way back in 1709. You may know the words by heart:

"Praise God from whom all blessings flow; praise Him, all creatures here below; praise Him above, ye heavenly host; praise Father, Son, and Holy Ghost."

Is there any more wonderful song for us to sing when we gather for worship? The word, "doxology", literally means "to speak or sing glory!" That's how the Lord's Prayer ends, just as it began, glorifying God. The same thing is true with the Shorter Catechism because we "glorify and enjoy God" (see Question 1) when we say, sing, or pray words of doxology. We're reminded of our "chief end," our primary purpose – to shine God's glory to the world in our thoughts, words, and actions. And His glorious purpose for us doesn't end here on the earth. One of the best things Christians will do in eternity is to join the saints, angels, and all the new creation in doxology to the Triune God. We'll join the heavenly choir, singing:

> "To him who sits on the throne and to the Lamb be blessing and honor and glory and might forever and ever!" (Revelation 5:13).

> "Hallelujah! For the Lord our God the Almighty reigns. Let us rejoice and exult and give Him the glory!" (Revelation 19:6-7).

Doxologies encourage us as we close our prayers because they celebrate our glorious and powerful King who alone hears and answers our prayers. And this eternal King who created all things is the same One who has loved us from before the foundation of the world, has sent His Son as our Redeemer, and has brought us eternal life through His Holy Spirit (Ephesians 1:3-14).

No wonder Jesus encourages us to end our prayers with Amen. This word means, "truly," or "so be it," or "may it be fulfilled."[23] When we add our amen to our prayers, we're trusting in Paul's comforting words:

---

23 Joseph Thayer, *Thayer's Greek-English Lexicon of the New Testament: Coded with Strong's Concordance Numbers* (Hendrickson Academic, Peabody, Mass) 1995, p. 32.

"For the Son of God, Jesus Christ....was not Yes and No, but in him it is always Yes. For all the promises of God find their Yes in him. That is why it is through him that we utter our Amen to God for his glory" (2 Corinthians 1:19-20).

May these final words of the catechism encourage each one of us, young and old, that God loves us in His Son Jesus Christ, and that His Spirit has empowered us to be living doxologies, "glorifying and enjoying Him," until He calls us home to join His heavenly choir.

CHALLENGE QUESTIONS:

- What doxologies do you sing in your church?
- Can you think of other doxologies in the Bible?
- How can we be "living doxologies," bringing glory to God?
- What does the word "Amen" mean and why do we end our prayers with it?

PRAYER:

Yours, O LORD, is the greatness and the power and the glory and the victory and the majesty, for all that is in the heavens and in the earth is yours. Yours is the kingdom, O LORD, and you are exalted as head above all (1 Chronicles 29:11). May you hear and answer our prayers and may our lives shine the light of Jesus Christ in our minds, voices, and actions. In His name we pray, Amen.

CHRISTIAN FOCUS IS FOR KIDS

CF4KIDS

That means you and your friends can all find a book to help you from the CF4KIDS range – from the very littlest baby to kids that are almost too old to be called a kid anymore.

We publish books that introduce you to the real Jesus, the truth of God's Word, and what that means for boys and girls of all ages.

Reading books is a fun way to find out what it is like to be a follower of Jesus Christ.

True stories, adventures, activity books, and devotions – they are all here for you and your family.

Christian Focus is part of the family of God. We aim to glorify Jesus and help you trust and follow Him.

Christian Focus Publications Ltd,
Geanies House, Fearn, Ross-shire, IV20 1TW, Scotland,
United Kingdom.
www.christianfocus.com